School exclusion and transition into adulthood in African-Caribbean communities

Also in this series

Young Turks and Kurds: A set of 'invisible' disadvantaged groups
Pinar Enneli, Tariq Modood and Harriet Bradley

Young Bangladeshi people's experience of transition to adulthood
Mairtin Mac an Ghaill and Chris Haywood

Life after care: The experiences of young people from different ethnic groups
Ravinder Barn, Linda Andrew and Nadia Mantovani

This publication can be provided in alternative formats, such as large print, Braille, audiotape and on disk. Please contact: Communications Department, Joseph Rowntree Foundation, The Homestead, 40 Water End, York YO30 6WP.
Tel: 01904 615905. Email: info@jrf.org.uk

School exclusion and transition into adulthood in African-Caribbean communities

*Cecile Wright, Penny Standen, Gus John,
Gerry German and Tina Patel*

JOSEPH ROWNTREE
FOUNDATION

The **Joseph Rowntree Foundation** has supported this project as part of its programme of research and innovative development projects, which it hopes will be of value to policy makers, practitioners and service users. The facts presented and views expressed in this report are, however, those of the authors and not necessarily those of the Foundation.

Joseph Rowntree Foundation
The Homestead
40 Water End
York YO30 6WP
Website: www.jrf.org.uk

ISBN 1 85935 349 5   (paperback)
ISBN 1 85935 350 9   (pdf: available at www.jrf.org.uk)

A CIP catalogue record for this report is available from the British Library.

Cover design by Adkins Design

Prepared and printed by:
York Publishing Services Ltd
64 Hallfield Road
Layerthorpe
York YO31 7ZQ
Tel: 01904 430033; Fax: 01904 430868; Website: www.yps-publishing.co.uk

Further copies of this report, or any other JRF publication, can be obtained either from the JRF website (www.jrf.org.uk/bookshop/) or from our distributor, York Publishing Services Ltd, at the above address.

Contents

Acknowledgements

The research reported was funded by Joseph Rowntree Foundation (JRF).

We wish to thank the researchers who have been involved in this study:
Dr Caroline Howarth, Sonia Davis, Dr Annecka Marshall, George Fisher and
Levi Heban. We would like to thank Dr Christine Callender, Sonia Thompson,
Vanessa Augusta, P.C. Gilbert, Tony Graham, Paul Grant, Anne Downie, Councillor
Des Wilson, Courtney Rose, Philip Hayes, Linda Wright, Steve Small, Kevin Brown
(formerly of Build), Michael Henry, Steve Philips, Cleveland Thompson, Kevin Brown
(Senior Youth Worker), Lee Jasper, Lee Parker, Rev. Hughie La Rose,
Sue Wheeldon, Yvonne Aubrey, Kate Dickson and Declan Gaffney for their support.
Thanks to all the members of the Advisory Panel: Diane Abbott, MP, Dr Maud Blair,
Professor Ann Phoenix, Veronica Price-Job, Hazel Simpson and Balbir Chatrik who
provided the authors with excellent support and advice during the research process.
We also thank Sandra Odell for providing vital administrative support throughout the
period of the project.

Thanks, too, must go to the young people and their families and carers, and the
many agencies that have worked with the young people following school exclusion.
Without their willingness to give so generously of their time and information this
study would not have been possible. All names have been changed to protect the
young people's anonymity.

And last but not least we would like to thank the staff at JRF: Marguerite Owen and
Charlie Lloyd, Principal Research Manager, for excellent inputs, suggestions,
thoughtfulness, encouragement and considerable support throughout the project.

Executive summary

■ In spite of a recent improvement in exclusion statistics for African-Caribbean children they are still over-represented in school exclusions. With only 15 per cent of permanently excluded young people reintegrated into mainstream school, successful transition into adulthood, employment and independence for most of these young people is unlikely.

■ Given the importance of education in achieving successful transitions and social inclusion, the research set out to examine the strategies developed by African-Caribbean young people excluded from school who achieve successful transitions and to discover how support from family, community and other agencies can lead to successful transitions for excluded young people.

■ Thirty-three young people from Nottingham and London took part in the study. They were between the ages of 14 and 19, born in the UK, with at least one parent of African-Caribbean descent and had experienced permanent exclusion or two fixed-term exclusions between the ages of 14 and 16. They were recruited from a wide range of community-based agencies.

■ Data were generated from over 100 interviews, which were carried out with the young people on a maximum of three occasions. Eighteen of these interviews were with family members, 12 from voluntary organisations (representing 19 organisations) and seven (representing four organisations) from the statutory sector.

■ Interviews with the young people revealed an inevitable suspicion of the reasons given for their exclusion and a sense of unfairness. Although they recognised that, in some cases, their behaviour did not conform to that expected in the traditional structured process of education and schooling, they believed that pressures on the school to meet performance targets had resulted in an inappropriate response. The contrast between the punishment allocated to their white counterparts for the same or even worse behaviour exacerbated their sense of unfairness.

■ For many, the exclusion had been a traumatic experience, which had led to a loss of dignity and self-respect and, for those in care, being excluded had been particular distressing. However, this loss of self-worth was an immediate and temporary reaction. In the vast majority of cases, it was followed by the development of a resilient sense of self, aided by adopting a black identity that motivated them to disprove official expectations of them and instead seek to create their own aspirations informed by the positiveness of their identity. In spite of their experiences, they remained committed to gaining an education.

- In some cases, the experience had a damaging effect on the young person's relationships with family members but, on the whole, they reported that their families believed in and emotionally supported them. Support was also found in relationships with friends and from sympathetic teachers, social workers, voluntary groups, the church and black community.

- A key theme was the exclusion representing a critical moment in the young person's life, which had created a change and awareness in their attitudes to issues around exclusion, racism and empowerment. This critical moment also led to a determination by the young people to change their behaviour in order to succeed in the attainment of educational qualifications and hence prove their worth.

- Over a third of interviewees moved to another school following their exclusion, although this may have been after a period without alternative educational provision. In spite of this, almost half had gained some qualifications, and at the time of interview, two-thirds were in further education and only three were unemployed.

- Factors identified by the young people as having been instrumental in facilitating successful transitions were the support of family and friends, emotional capital, social and cultural capital, access to resources and provision, class and economic capital, determination to overcome the exclusion label and educational opportunities.

- For the families of the young people, the experience of exclusion was as painful as it was for the young people themselves.

- On the whole, the family members interviewed expressed positive views about the young person's school before the exclusion. After the experience of appeals and panel meetings, although the young people's families had continued to believe in the value of education, they had developed negative views of it. However, in response to the state of educational limbo in which their relative was left, they sought to empower themselves through seeking help from voluntary community organisations, through the process of appeals against the exclusion and by demanding educational rights for the young people.

- Families had largely believed the young person's version of events leading up to the exclusion and expressed their support by helping them with learning and accessing and using resources, acting as advocates, providing positive emotional support and expressing their belief in the young person.

- For some of the families, teachers were helpful but, for the majority, they had been unhelpful and hostile. On the whole, they found the support from statutory resources to be inadequate while support from voluntary organisations had been viewed as particularly beneficial. These not only provided emotional support and advice for both the young person and the relative, but also helped with appeal meetings. Extended family members have also been found to be a valuable source of help, assistance and guidance.

- None of the agencies whose representatives were interviewed was set up specifically to help young people who had been excluded from school. Most had only short-term funding and workers, some of whom had themselves been excluded from school, were extremely dedicated to their jobs, often working long hours.

- The types of support offered by the representatives of the agencies interviewed included practical help, such as: providing an alternative learning site; helping with reintegration into mainstream education; giving advice about careers and employment; and assisting with advocacy and representation. In addition, most of them provided emotional support and guidance, and aimed to help the young people with positive identity formation and improving family relationships.

- They saw their work as filling a vacuum created by the shortcomings of statutory service provision and for the lack of support they provided for young people and families. A common theme was the importance of the community in providing an alternative educational site that would also help to redress the racism they encountered within the education system.

- In making recommendations for future policy, it is recognised that the study sample was limited in that it was obtained through agencies that had been supporting the young people and that many young people most at risk after school exclusion are those who receive no support. However, our focus was on the strategies that enable young people to make successful transitions following school exclusion. A strength of the study was the collection of material from different sources using the young person as the starting point and asking them to nominate other people we should interview.

■ Recommendations include: changing the ways in which education for 13 to 19 year olds is resourced and organised to facilitate the movement of young people between institutions in their search to find a method of education appropriate to their requirements; promoting partnership working between the education services and the youth service, and between the education services and the voluntary and community sectors, and between the education services and parents, ensuring that, when difficulties at school arise, intervention is initiated swiftly to avoid the escalation of the situation and long periods without educational provision, which would infringe the young person's rights.

1 Background to the study

In spite of a recent improvement in exclusion statistics for African-Caribbean children, they are still over-represented in school exclusions. Given the importance of education in successful transition to adulthood and social inclusion, we need to know where current services fail to effectively meet the needs of this group and where adjustments can be made. This report aims to address this lack of information by examining the experiences of excluded young African-Caribbean people and specifically how they develop strategies that enable successful transitions following school exclusion.

The findings of the research reported here provide data, which can inform both central and local government policy on school exclusion as well as meet the requirement for local government to have information on the status of young African-Caribbean people in the local population. The findings are also useful to voluntary and community organisations assessing the effectiveness of local partnerships in reducing social exclusion and enabling inclusion.

To provide the context for the study, Chapter 1 provides a brief review of the literature on transition to adulthood and specifically how social class, gender and race and ethnicity are key factors influencing the nature of youth transitions. It also examines the role of education in successful transitions and the extent and significance of school exclusion for African-Caribbean people, along with the policy contexts and initiatives to promote inclusion and successful transition. Although the authors of this report favour the use of the term 'African-Caribbean' to refer to people of Caribbean heritage, the term 'black' is often used interchangeably, especially when reporting the work of others who have used this term. This chapter concludes with a description of how the study was carried out.

The remainder of the report has been structured to ensure that the research findings themselves constitute the central focus of the document, with each of the three main chapters focusing on specific aspects of the research. Wherever possible, we have used the narratives of the participants to illustrate the issues discussed.

Chapter 2 presents data obtained from interviews with the young people. Chapter 3 presents information from family and carers. Chapter 4 presents the perspective of voluntary and community organisations that have worked with the young person following school exclusion. A number of case studies are also presented focusing on the nature of the work with young people.

In Chapter 5, the key research findings are considered. This chapter will make a number of recommendations for schools, local education authorities (LEAs), and central and local government for reducing the involvement of young people in school and social exclusionary processes and to acknowledge the crucial role that the black voluntary and community sector can play in this.

Review of the literature

Understanding transitions

The nature of the influences affecting how young people make the transition to adulthood is multifaceted (e.g. Jones, 2002; Thomson *et al.*, 2002). These transitions can consist of a single change or combination of changes that can involve any of the following: participation in the labour market, having an adult income, economic independence, secure housing, or being a partner, spouse or parent (e.g. Jones, 2002). However, one can be defined as an adult in one sense, e.g. being a parent, but not in another, e.g. still living with one's parents (Jones, 2002).

Since the 1990s, there has been a considerable change in the nature of youth transitions. There is now much more variation in youth transitions as a result of the change in the labour market (e.g. Ahier and Moore, 1999). In the 1970s, two-thirds of young people left school at age 16 and the vast majority fairly quickly gained full-time jobs. Changes to the economy have now meant that poorly qualified young people take unskilled jobs offering low pay, poor training and job insecurity, and qualified young people take the better-paid jobs with greater security (Green *et al.*, 2001). These changes, along with the growth of higher education, have resulted in it becoming more difficult for young people to become independent (Bynner, 2001).

Young people now continue for longer in full-time education, realising that entry to the labour market is increasingly dependent on higher skills and qualifications. The staying-on rate is higher for African-Caribbean young people than for white young people, but participation in degree study is lower (DfES, 2003b). This disproportionately high staying on rate by minority ethnic groups involves a rather complex picture in that this group is less likely to be found in the more 'prestigious' universities. This group is also more likely to achieve lower classes of degrees on average than white young people. In turn, this adversely affects their progression into the labour market, as larger employers are found to be more likely to recruit individuals from the more 'prestigious' universities (DfES, 2003d).

School exclusion, social exclusion and African-Caribbean people

Official statistics on exclusion from school have tended to define school exclusion in terms of a fixed period with the pupil readmitted afterwards or a permanent exclusion where the pupil is removed from the school roll. However, it is recognised that official statistics on exclusion may omit a significant number of unofficial or unrecorded exclusions, both permanent and fixed-term (Osler *et al.*, 2002). Additionally, it is not always clear whether figures refer to permanent or fixed-term exclusions. This must be borne in mind when reviewing the literature. However, there is general agreement when examining those groups considered to be vulnerable to exclusion, particularly permanent exclusions, that there is a disproportionately high rate of exclusion among young people of African-Caribbean background (Ofsted, 2001). This is particularly true for boys with African-Caribbean heritage who are between four and 15 times more likely to be excluded than white boys, depending on locality (Sewell, 1997; DfEE, 2000a). African-Caribbean girls are four times more likely to be permanently excluded than white girls (Osler *et al.*, 2002).

Given the increasing importance of education to successful youth transitions, what is the impact of school exclusion on the experience of transition for these young people? In recent years, there has been an overall improvement in the relative position of African-Caribbean children in the exclusion statistics. In 1997, 0.78 per cent of African-Caribbean children were permanently excluded. Although, by 2001/02, the proportion had fallen to 0.4 per cent, the figure for white children was still much lower at 0.13 per cent and, by 2002/03, permanent exclusions for African-Caribbean children fell further to 0.25 compared to the proportionately lower figure of 0.12 for white children. Hence, despite the improvement, African-Caribbean children are still substantially more likely to be excluded (DfES, 2003b, 2004).

The disproportionate exclusion of African-Caribbean young people from schools has prompted Ofsted (2001) to comment that the reasons:

> ... are rarely clear cut, but many Black pupils who find themselves subject to disciplinary procedures perceive themselves to have been unfairly treated ... Black pupils were more likely to be excluded for what was defined by schools as 'challenging behaviour'. The length of fixed term exclusions varied considerably in the same school between Black and white pupils for what are described as the same or similar incidents. (Ofsted, 2001, p. 20)[1]

A number of studies show that African-Caribbean young people excluded from school have not usually exhibited 'disruptive' behaviour prior to attending secondary school and are not usually disaffected with education (e.g. Gillborn and Gipps, 1996; Wright *et al.*, 2000; Blair, 2001). At primary school, the achievement of African-Caribbean children is often higher at Key Stage 1 than other groups but attainment declines in relation to other groups so that, at Key Stage 4 (age 16), it is among the lowest (Osler and Hill, 1999). These changes mean that transition pathways for many African-Caribbean young people will be more severely constrained than for other groups.

Further, with only 15 per cent of permanently excluded young people being reintegrated into mainstream school (DfEE, 2000a), successful transition into adulthood, employment and independence for most of these young people is unlikely.

It has long been noted that there is a link between those who have been excluded from school and social exclusion in later life. For many excluded children, a transition into adulthood becomes a transition into social and psychological insecurity (Parsons and Castle, 1999). Permanent exclusion is often associated with long periods without education and underachievement, reduced employment opportunities, entry to crime, a greater likelihood of becoming a teenage parent and inaccessibility to social resources.[2]

Family and community involvement in schooling and transitions

There is a long tradition of self-help or community-led initiatives in shaping the transitional experience of young black people (Weekes and Wright, 1998; Rhamie and Hallam, 2002). These initiatives can be viewed as a response to an education system that is perceived by the black community as victimising and pathologising young black people and representing them as underachievers and anti-education. They reflect notions of self-help and empowerment. 'Social capital' is central to this strategy for empowering ordinary people. This is in the sense of social capital as consisting of networks of co-operation and reciprocity, civic engagement and strong community identity (Bourdieu, 1986; Putnam, 1995).

Initiatives such as supplementary schools and community mentoring programmes have historically embodied the application of black social and cultural capital within the context of education and transition. Supplementary schools are part-time voluntary schools occurring either after school or on a Saturday. They provide a black-dominated environment in which black children can learn (DfES, 2003c). They focus on the curriculum, reinforcing particular cultures, enhancing young people's self-respect, promoting self-discipline and inspiring young people to have high aspirations to succeed academically (Dove, 1993; Reay and Mirza, 1997). Community-run mentoring programmes, by and for the black community, aim to help young people build a confident self-identity and assist in the planning of educational and successful career goals. Schemes such as the black mentor schemes in Southwark, KWESI, AFWI and 100 Black Men in Birmingham and the Windsor Fellowship in London are nationally renowned (Weekes and Wright, 1998; Appiah, 2001).

In the literature on black parental involvement it is observed that mothers provide emotional support for children's academic success (Reay, 2000). It has been shown that mothers equip their children with strategies to assist them in overcoming institutional racism (Reay and Mirza, 1997; Reynolds, 2001). The literature further suggests that, for young black people, the alternative spheres of community networks, the voluntary sector and family relationships encourage a positive identity and sense of community in the face of enduring structures of race and class inequalities (Alleyne, 2002).

All the above illustrate the variety of attempts by families and community organisations to assist young black people to achieve successful transitions. Recently, social policy has recognised the importance of cultural resources in black communities as a means of building social cohesion and achieving inclusion. The Government is therefore recognising the values and skills in the community, and is attempting to engage the black and minority ethnic sector in efforts to address social exclusion (SEU, 1999; Home Office, 2002; DfES, 2003c).

Policy context, response and national initiatives for young people

A variety of policies and measures exist with the intention of increasing the proportion of young people who will take the education/training route after 16. These include Educational Maintenance Allowances, Excellence in Cities, Sure Start and the Learning Gateway, delivered via Connexions.[3]

In essence, in relation to youth transitions, government policy clearly prioritises education and training as the 'successful' route. The measures outlined above aim to keep young people in school as far as possible, in keeping with the overall strategy of social inclusion. Many young people still see the transition to adulthood as being primarily through work or employment and not via more education or training, and there is relatively little in policy initiatives that focuses on vocational training. Similarly, there are still significant policy gaps in relation to the needs of specific groups, e.g. school excludees who have now left school, those working-class young people with relatively little high-value social or cultural capital to enable successful transitions and, of course, in the context of this report, the needs of African-Caribbean young people and other ethnic groups.

This research aims to provide data on young African-Caribbean people who have been excluded from school. The impact of school exclusions on youth transitions for young people of African-Caribbean heritage has received little attention. Likewise, there is an absence of studies focusing on how young people develop strategies that enable successful transitions following school exclusion.

Systematic school-exclusion procedures have been in place for 18 years, yet exclusions still feature significantly in the experiences of schools, pupils and their families. Despite research reports, DfES initiatives and advice and guidance, exclusion is frequently used as a punitive measure rather than as a last resort.(Blair, 2001). Much depends on a school's access to essential resources, staff development and training to prevent exclusion.

Research focus and methodology

Aims

- To develop an understanding of what school exclusion might mean to those involved and how it might impact on the experience of youth transition of African-Caribbean people.

- Examine the strategies developed by African-Caribbean young people excluded from school who achieve successful transitions.

- Discover how support from family, community and other agencies can lead to successful transitions for excluded young people.

- Provide a voice for excluded African-Caribbean young people and those who support them.

The research focus

The research has focused on the perspectives of young people, families or carers and community organisations primarily to give them a voice in the debate about exclusion, inclusion and transitions. Adopting a multifocal approach, we wanted to know what the young people, their families and community organisations could tell us about what worked in reducing social exclusion and enabling inclusion, and what insights might be provided with respect to community and family strategies. According to the literature, these young people constituted a potentially difficult group to engage with the research process. Allen (2002) asserts that vulnerable young people have been under-represented in research owing to a number of methodological and ethical problems.

Location of study

The research was conducted in two cities: Nottingham and London.

Nottingham

The black population of the city of Nottingham has increased by 40 per cent since the 1991 census to 17,419 in 2001. This represents 6.5 per cent of the total population of the city. Nearly 40 per cent of the population of the city is under the age of 25. This is a much higher proportion than the national average. The level of underachievement among children of African-Caribbean background is high and so is the level of exclusion. However, figures available do not distinguish between permanent or fixed-term exclusions. In 2001/02, nearly 25 per cent of the black[4] (see the beginning of this chapter for a definition of 'black') pupils were excluded, compared with under 11 per cent of the non-black population. Black pupils were therefore more than twice as likely to be excluded. The corresponding figure for Asian pupils was just over 4 per cent; and, for white pupils, 16 per cent (Nottingham City Council Education Department, 2002).[5] There is a high unemployment and social disconnection among school leavers, with African-Caribbean men being particularly affected (findings from the cross-programme evaluation 2002/03, Radford and Hyson Green New Deal for Communities).

London

Between 1991 and 2001, the white population of London decreased while that for all major minority ethnic groups increased. The African-Caribbean population increased by 18 per cent in this period but this was less than any other major minority ethnic group. Forty-eight per cent of under 18s in London are non-white compared with 9 per cent for the UK as a whole. African-Caribbean under 18s form 15 per cent of all children in London. About half of these children live in income poverty (Howes,

2003). In 1999, only 37 per cent of black pupils (the statistics refer to young people of both Caribbean and African heritage) achieved five or more GCSEs at grades A*–C compared with 50 per cent of white pupils and 62 per cent of Indian pupils. London has a high permanent exclusion rate – 0.16 per cent of pupils. The exclusion rate for white pupils is slightly more than the national average (0.15 per cent compared with 0.14 per cent); for Asians it is slightly less than the national average (0.06 per cent compared with 0.07 per cent). However, it is still the case that the exclusion rate for black pupils is much higher than the national average and higher than the other groups (0.27 per cent), compared with 0.15 per cent for whites and 0.06 per cent for Asians (DfES, 2003a).

Participants

A sample of 33 young people (21 male, 12 female) between the ages of 14 and 19 who had experienced permanent school exclusion were recruited to the study: 20 from London and 13 from Nottingham. In London, the young people were recruited through the Communities Empowerment Network (CEN) and the Intensive Supervision and Surveillance Programme (ISSP). In Nottingham, the young people were recruited from a wide range of agencies that primarily represented community-based projects for initiatives for working with young black people (see Appendix 6). These organisations were asked to contact young people who met the following criteria:

■ aged between 14 and 19

■ had experienced permanent exclusion or two fixed-term exclusions between the ages of 14 and 16

■ must have been born in the UK

■ had at least one parent of African-Caribbean descent.

If, having been informed of the study, the young people were happy to be involved, their details were passed to the research team and a member of the team contacted them to arrange an introductory interview. The characteristics of the young people who took part are shown in Appendix 1.

Data collected

Data were to be collected through four activities.

1   *An introductory interview with young people*: to enable the construction of their story of school exclusion and transition, and the identification of family member(s)/significant other(s)/friend(s) who had supported them during the period of exclusion and beyond, and who could be approached to take part in the study. In the introductory meetings, young people were given disposable cameras to document how school exclusions had changed their lives. It was hoped that bringing the photographs to the second interview would enable the young people to discuss important issues raised in the photographs with the help of their friends (Clark and Moss, 2001).

2   *A friendship group interview*: those young people who had taken part in the first interview were contacted for a second interview once sufficient time had elapsed for them to take their photographs. They were offered the option of bringing along their own self-selected friendship group. Topics to be explored included systems of support, identity and resistance.

3   *Final interview with young people*: approximately ten months after the initial interview with the young person, a final interview would take place in order to elicit information about how they had changed in the intervening months and their aspiration for the future. It was also hoped that repeated contact with the young person would facilitate the articulation of their account.

4   *Interviews with family members/carers and significant others*: these focused primarily on how they supported the young person through the process of exclusion and their transition to maturity.

All interviews were recorded onto audiotape. For a variety of reasons it was not possible to complete all three interviews for each young person. However, 13 young people from Nottingham took part in at least one interview as did 20 young people from London. Details of the interview dataset collected are shown in Appendix 2.

Analysis

For reasons of accuracy, all the interviews were transcribed before being analysed according to guidelines suggested by Smith and Osbourn (2003). They advocate a systematic approach involving methodically working through a transcript in order to identify themes and categories. These are then progressively integrated until 'master themes' are established that capture the essence of the subject matter.

2 Young people's accounts of exclusion and transition

Ray (18), Nottingham

Ray is of mixed-heritage background and has been in residential care from the age of three. At the time of the study, he was living in a supported home and was in regular contact with his maternal grandfather. He has attended a number of special schools and has been excluded several times, the first of which was when he was in primary school. By the age of 14 he had experienced a number of fixed-term exclusions, which led ultimately to a permanent exclusion. The official reasons offered for his exclusions included disruptive behaviour, fighting and assaulting a teacher. Ray felt that officials, teachers and the school often ignored the bullying he was subjected to from other children because he was in care and it was the bullying that caused him to be involved in fights. He felt that teachers then unfairly blamed him for the incidents believing that, because he was in care, he was violent. The pattern of school exclusion had seriously disrupted his education, as he had been unable to study for GCSEs.

During the periods of exclusion from school, Ray received consistent support from his social worker, who advocated on his behalf and renegotiated his return to school and ultimately a place at the local college. He also received support from his foster family, grandfather, best friend and a local black voluntary organisation.

He is currently in full-time education studying basic literacy and numeracy and a course in drama at the local college.

Introduction

This chapter presents the young people's retrospective accounts of their experiences of school exclusion and transitions into adulthood. It does so by identifying patterns and trends, but also what is idiosyncratic for the young people. The chapter explores the meaning and the effects of the exclusion, and how the exclusion experience and being labelled as troublesome plays a large role in the young person's perception of self. It also outlines their development of a strong positive self-definition in their attempt to overcome the exclusion reputation and to counteract the processes of racialisation that they are likely to face in wider society. Additional themes identified by the young people include the exclusion from school as a critical moment in their lives and the value of family, friends and the African-Caribbean community as sources of support in creating positive outcomes.

Perceptions of the reasons for the exclusion

Table 1 presents what the young people reported as the principal reason their school gave for the exclusion. In their view, the reasons they were given by their school focused on their own problematic nature, specifically their challenging behaviour. The reasons are listed in Table 1 together with the frequency with which they were reported.

However, 19 of the young people disagreed with the reason they felt the school had given them and suggested that what really lay behind their exclusion was: the increasing pressure on schools to gain a high position in exam-result league tables and reach government targets; the increasingly academic nature of the curriculum, which made it difficult for pupils who fell behind to catch up; insufficient support for pupils with behavioural difficulties; and tensions in teacher–pupil relationships:

> I'm trying to make you understand the climate of the school. The exclusions were coming in fast and furious for anything ... because Ofsted people were there.
> (Sirita, 16, London)

Table 1 Young people's perceptions of the reasons for the exclusion

Reason	Total
Attitude problems	4
Behavioural problems, including disruptive behaviour	6
Stealing	1
Graffiti	1
Violent behaviour, including fighting, verbal abuse, aggressive behaviour	11
Truancy	1
Bullying	1
Smoking cannabis	1
Forgery	1
Unknown	6
Total	33

Similarly, Lee had said:

> … before all this happened yeah when he *[headmaster]* come in the first year he said he wants to get rid of all like the people I hang around with so at the end of the year yeah he suspended like all of my friends and said it's early study leave yeah, but everyone else is at school apart from my friends so they knew they were suspended but he tried saying it's study leave so parents were phoning in complaining.
> (Lee, 16, London)

This had meant that some young people viewed their exclusion as unjust or as a punishment for something that they were innocent of:

> I wasn't actually there at the time, but instantly I'm the culprit … I thought it was kind of funny that the teacher tried to accuse me when it was a white guy in a red coat and I'm black in a blue coat! In that kind of sense it was amusing but it wasn't really because they were trying to get me for it.
> (David, 17, Nottingham)

Similarly Latisha had reported:

> I got accused of bullying … no one saw me do anything … I just got excluded.
> (Latisha, 18, Nottingham)

Many of the interviewees recognised that their exclusion may have resulted from their failure to conform to the traditional structured process of education and schooling but, even for those young people who admit a wrongdoing, there is still a sense of unfairness in being labelled inaccurately:

> I weren't the only person … I admit yeah, I might have been talking … but it's not like if the room was silent and I was talking. Everybody was talking and I just got picked out. That's the way it seemed to me. I was the one what got caught yeah.
> (Antoine, 16, London)

The excluded young person's sense of unfairness at the exclusion was exacerbated when they compared what had happened to them with the punishment allocated to their white counterparts for the same, or similar, or even worse behaviour:

> If I was white I might have got away with it possibly.
> (Richard, 18, Nottingham)

Similarly, Lucinda had said:

> I think it's because I'm black, especially how the other *[white]* girl was
> allowed back to school the next day.
> (Lucinda, 17, London)

Earl had specifically identified the ways in which the teachers' behaviour fostered
racial divisions:

> … they play the white kids against the black ones, being a white child or
> something, the black child gets in trouble for it and the white child gets
> away with it, you see them do it and the black child gets in trouble for it.
> (Earl, 18, Nottingham)

Stereotypical expectations of African-Caribbean young people as troublemakers,
challenging and aggressive have been widely documented (Mirza, 1992; Gillborn
and Gipps, 1996; Wright *et al.*, 1998). The young people in this study also felt
trapped by the white teachers' and white pupils' low expectations and understanding
of black culture, and their stereotypes of black students as aggressive, athletic and
oversized. Ray and Melona reported experiences of such stigmatisation:

> I felt that because of my size yes and because of my colour, because
> when they see a black person in their face they feel intimidated.
> (Ray, 18, Nottingham)

And:

> … anything I do in school like they bang down on it that's how I see it
> because I'm black as well they just think that's just another black naughty
> kid … but because I got brains and I'm smarter than most students in my
> school year they can't do that … they just associated me as one of the
> black kids yeah not like she's a smart child she can do her work she's
> talented and this way or whatever and they never ever picked up on that
> they just thought that's a black child come down on it hard as they want it
> out basically, they tried their hardest but they couldn't get me out.
> (Melona, 16, London)

Having been previously temporarily excluded made this labelling more likely:

> There was even one point that a teacher was like 'ah you're Lucinda, I've
> heard a lot about you', like things like that … *[after that]* I felt demotivated.
> (Lucinda, 17, London)

And, once a label was acquired, it was difficult to shake it off:

> ... she *[teacher]* would automatically think it was me because it would usually be me, but on this particular time it wasn't me ... but I think this one lesson I was actually being good and then I was wrongfully blamed ... it's like I had made a name for myself and then it wasn't me ... I remember one time a teacher did say they used to talk about me in the staffroom.
> (David, 17, Nottingham)

Altogether, nearly half of the young people believed that racism or racial stereotyping had played a role in their exclusion from school. It should be noted that no differences were found between the reports of those with one white parent and those where both parents were black. Both groups were treated as 'black':

> ... it's just the way those people *[teachers]* see us, the young black males of today they *[the teachers]* see them with their trousers falling down, into the violence, us young girls having babies. So they think we haven't got much.
> (Sirita, 16, London)

The young people also felt that they had been stereotyped in other ways; for example, one young man who had been in care reported:

> If I had one fight with someone else they would blame me and saw me as the violent one ... I don't know ... the teachers just looked at me like this, 'oh he's in a children's home and he's got no family so he's out of control'.
> (Ray, 18, Nottingham)

The aftermath of the exclusion and its influence on life at school

Being excluded from school labels the excludee as unteachable and undeserving of an education. This has a detrimental effect on the excludee who, despite having misgivings about the behaviour of teachers and the school's attitude, wants to return to school in order to continue their education or be with friends:

> The worst part was the meetings that I had to go to because he *[teacher]* basically just said that I was lying and that I had to tell the truth or I was never going to come back and that I had to admit to hitting the teacher

and that I attacked and stuff like that. I can remember just crying and crying and crying and he's like you're not coming back until you apologise and I was like after two days of being excluded, two or three days of the exclusion and I had a meeting on Monday morning and he said 'well you're not coming back because you're not sorry enough'. I thought I was coming back to school as I was all dressed in my uniform, had my books and I was just shattered.
(Tamara, 15, London)

Even when reinstatement had been achieved, the difficulty of reintegration meant that the excludees were very rarely able to learn on a basis equal to other pupils. Despite their efforts to catch up, some did not find their reinstatement into the school that had excluded them successful:

> ... sometimes they would give me a piece of work and they would leave me with that for the whole day and nothing else. Then it came to the stage that it was breaktimes and I was not allowed to have breaktimes. When it came to lunchtimes, I had to come out of the premises, and they were treating it like a prison.
> (Paul, 16, London)

Many interviewees explained that they were ostracised when they attempted to reintegrate in schools. They suffered from being ignored by both teachers and other students, who perceived them as troublemakers and liars. Some teachers were very reluctant to teach them and expressed open hostility:

> ... after *[the exclusion]* I felt I was labelled and picked on by teachers, especially the headmaster, for little incidents ... when I got back yeah he would just stop me for anything.
> (Lee, 16, London)

Often the other pupils refused to speak to them:

> I hated that school so much I was determined to leave because they turned the kids against me, 'oh stay away from Bernard'.
> (Bernard, 19, Nottingham)

Having no access to education left some with nothing to do and nowhere to go, which led to them getting caught up in committing offending behaviour when excluded:

> ... it's hard because being out of school leads to committing crime
> because you're out of school and ain't got nothing to do ... and what I'm
> saying is that the kind of person I am, I am easily misled by friends ...
> because I'm free ... I don't live at home with my mum, I live in a children's
> home.
> (Will, 15, London)

Just under half of the young people interviewed had been involved in offending
behaviour: 15 of them reported having received either a conviction or a caution (see
case study for Will below).

Will (London)

Will is a 15-year-old young man who has been excluded from school for
disruptive behaviour three times. When Will was 12 years old he was accused of
making a sexual comment to a teacher and permanently excluded. Will
describes the hardship of being labelled, forced out of the school for two years
and trying to get an education. He maintains that the barriers to finding a tutor
and going to a centre are extremely difficult. Will claims that having nothing
constructive to do has led to his involvement in criminal activities. He is learning
from his mistakes and staying out of trouble with the early intervention of the
Intervention Supervision and Surveillance Programme (ISSP).

Will asserts that school exclusion led to family breakdown because his mother
could not cope. Will's mother hit him, he ran away and has been living in
children's homes. Will is not in contact with his family and does not pay much
attention to the staff at the children's home. ISSP Youth Offenders' Team is
helping him to realise his goal to go to a centre or to college and do GCSEs. Will
states that it will be hard to catch up with his education and is aware of his
reduced job prospects without GCSEs. He thinks that he has the commitment to
overcome these obstacles and become self-employed.

Effects of being excluded on self-esteem and identity formation

For many, exclusion from school was a traumatic experience, which they felt was a
personal attack leading to a loss of dignity and respect. For example, Yolan had recalled:

> I went through a phase where [I was] really depressed and I didn't want
> to go back ... I just felt bad and I felt like I was unwanted sort of thing ...
> like I was just a reject of the school.
> (Yolan, 15, London)

These feelings were expressed by both male and female interviewees, and by those with both or only one African-Caribbean parent. However, for those in care, being excluded had been particularly distressing. For example, Ray had talked in depth about his feelings of growing up in a care home and his perception of how he thought others at the school had viewed him, in addition to the racial labels they had placed on him. This had clearly had an initial negative affect on his self-awareness:

> ... it's the way people look at me ... they *[teachers]* would blame my home ... and when they see me they are like scared of me when I am talking to them, and it's like 'I can't talk to him, he's a black youth, I'm better moving away' kind of thing.
> (Ray, 18, Nottingham)

However, for most, this loss of self-worth is a temporary reaction. In the vast majority of cases, it was followed by the development of a resilient sense of self:

> I think what I've been through has brought me to how I am now. I mean, if I didn't go through, what I've been through makes me who I am and I wouldn't be the way I am if I didn't go through what I went through. I think it taught me a lesson. I think I learnt quite a few lessons about myself ... I was really, really bad, but my experiences helped me to change, made me who I am now.
> (Matthew, 19, Nottingham)

Resistance to the experience was quite often driven by a desire to 'prove teachers wrong':

> ... my mum and dad just said, when I was excluded they just said ... the main thing ... was to turn the negative into a positive in the long run by what I did, what I achieved, my exam results, which was basically like spitting in the headteacher's face.
> (Roger, 15, London)

A consequence of the young people being judged negatively was that they turned this around to develop a positive sense of themselves. This maturity, independence and responsibility made the young people more focused on their studies and career prospects. For example, Leon had said:

> I want a decent job ... and anything that pays ... then look for an office job when I get a bit older like and wear suit and tie and everything ... it's not like I'm dumb ... I got plans. I got ideas for the future.
> (Leon, 16, London)

School exclusion as a reflection of processes likely to be experienced in wider society

Having confronted the negative way they had been portrayed through being excluded, the young people became aware that their experiences of school exclusion are more than likely to be mirrored in the world outside education. Thus this experience made them conscious of racialised practices that they will very likely experience in wider society (e.g. Gillborn and Mirza, 2000):

> ... it's a stereotype. I mean they will see us, they will see a group of black youths with fists up, they think that we're up to trouble straightaway. But sometimes it's not even like that, not up to trouble at all. But, because the colour of our skin because we've got hoods on and stuff, I mean they just stereotype us basically.
> (Nelson, 16, London)

Trying to compensate for the prejudice of others was something they felt was especially unfair:

> ... if you want to go somewhere you have to dress normal, if you've got hoods and trainers on people think you are out to cause trouble. Sometimes when I go into town and I've got jeans on and an ordinary coat they don't follow me *[security guards in the shop]*. As soon as I go in with my hoods and trainers they come heavy. It's like that every time ... I don't want to wear normal clothes. I want to wear what I like, why should I change my appearance for other people ... I have to be happy in my clothes.
> (Keenan, 18, Nottingham)

This was particularly difficult for those who were also attempting to overcome a criminal past. For example, despite having dealt with and overcome the negative aspects of the school exclusion, Christopher reported continued victimisation by the police:

> ... they *[police]* said I was supposed to have robbed someone ... because I have been arrested for it before, they are saying that it's my description ... but I know loads of people who can pass for the same description.
> (Christopher, 17, Nottingham)

For some, this awareness of the stereotypes around black culture had led to a desire to contest and resist the labels of unworthiness, being problematic and unteachable:

> I think that being black and that the reception that you get from other people sometimes it affects you and it can either make you weaker or stronger and I think in my case it has made me stronger … I just want to prove them wrong and I want to show them that they can stereotype as much as they like but that at the end of the day it's not necessarily true.
> (Tamara, 15, London)

However, despite their defiance of the stereotypical image of a school excludee, they acknowledged the possibility of continued exclusion by mainstream society in one form or another:

> … sometimes I think they don't think much of me because it's sometimes the look that I get … I've had people follow me round the shop … it's like they think immediately that I'm gonna steal somethink and I really hate that … so I don't think I'm seen very highly by other people.
> (Tamara, 15, London)

Prospects for employment

Exclusion from school has been found to hinder successful transitions into adulthood in the areas of employability and career development. According to Will:

> … it's a downfall for a job.
> (Will, 15, London)

This is primarily because the lack of educational qualifications is seen as a barrier in the competitive nature of today's labour market. As a result, the excluded young people feel that they are limited in their ability to apply for certain jobs:

> … obviously when you go for a job they always ask you what your school is and what qualification you have. If you ain't got none, or can't remember like your last school, that's bad.
> (Antoine, 16, London)

The interviewees recognised that entry to the labour market is increasingly dependent on higher skills and qualifications:

> … go back to college, go to school and don't get kicked out. It's not good in the long run … it's hard to find a decent job without qualifications.
> (Keenan, 18, Nottingham)

However, excluded young people have been shown to continue to exhibit high levels of optimism in terms of finding work and achieving career aspirations, which in turn helps them to gain control over their transition into employment (Rudd and Evans, 1998). For example, Earl, who had discussed his NVQ in music technology and his plans to do a two-year music course at college, had said:

> I am going to put my head down and get a career in music, and get a proper job.
> (Earl, 18, Nottingham)

This optimism was more likely to be realised by those whose families had the economic status through which the young person could access particular resources. For example, David, who had described himself as 'middle class', had recalled how his parents had been able to buy him a PC so that he could develop his music skills:

> … well my mum and stepdad bought me a PC *[personal computer]* so I can like make music at home and that. So they are actually spending money to help me progress.
> (David, 17, Nottingham)

Whatever their economic status, most of the young people attempted to counteract any limitation in choice by using the available resources around them and their own self-determination to enhance their options. They primarily did this by going back into mainstream education, going into further or higher education, or taking part in specialist training courses. All these pathways are embarked on by the young people with the long-term view of their completion increasing the young person's employability and career development:

> I've done my work experience and I'm doing business and finance now …
> I want to go to university and study a degree in business and finance.
> Then hopefully get a job like in financial services or an accountant or something in that area.
> (Lucinda, 17, London)

Relationships with others

The experience of exclusion can also have serious effects on the young person's relationships with family members (Cohen and Hughes, 1994, quoted in Parsons, 1999), peers and school friends (Pomeroy, 2000). In extreme cases, it can even precipitate a breakdown in relationships between the young person and their family:

> I went to the exclusion meetings ... but she *[mother]* was just like 'it's not my fault, I don't know why he did this' ... she was just making herself not to be a bad mother ... after that I just put myself into care, I couldn't live with my mum.
> (Anthony, 18, Nottingham)

However, such cases are few, with the vast majority of young people reporting that the exclusion experience and the family support later offered had led to an improvement in familial relationships:

> ... she *[mother]* believed me. I think it might have brought us closer together because she actually believed me and trusted me.
> (David, 17, Nottingham)

The excluded young people had found that they had received a huge amount of sympathy, understanding and support from their friends:

> I felt kind of happy. I thought they *[friends]* were just going to sit back and see what happened like, but they come and helped me without me asking them to come.
> (Lee, 16, London)

However, for some, their relationships with peers had been under strain, particularly the ability to make and continue relationships:

> I felt horrible because I was making friends and everything and then you have to leave all your friends behind, because I've never been able to make friends because I leave schools.
> (Ray, 18, Nottingham)

Exclusion as a critical moment

Individual circumstances and life events, or what Thomson *et al.* (2002) term 'critical moments', are significant in how particular young people follow a specific transition pathway. The exclusion as a critical moment had been experienced in very similar ways and had similar meanings for the young people, regardless of their class or African-Caribbean backgrounds. For a few young people, the exclusion had been viewed as a welcome break from the confines of the education system, their particular school or their victimisation by teachers and peers:

> ... it was a terrible school ... it was rubbish ... *[when excluded]* I loved it ... I didn't like that school, I didn't want to go back.
> (Kelly, 19, Nottingham)

For some, the exclusion represented a critical moment in their life, which had created a change and awareness in their attitudes to issues around exclusion, racism and empowerment:

> I think that, because I'm black, I have to try extra harder than my white counterparts especially and because of what happened to me within school as well, people can refer back to that and say 'yes' and use that as a justification for labelling me in the future ... so I have to work that bit extra to avoid it.
> (Roger, 15, London)

They also developed a more responsible and mature attitude in terms of their outlook on their own life. In doing so they gain control of the direction of their transition into adulthood:

> I would say I'm more mature and I would not do some of the things that I have done in the past ... I do want to succeed ... I'm more focused now ... in what I want to achieve. That's how I survived the exclusion.
> (Richard, 18, Nottingham)

The critical moment of the exclusion also led to changes in the young people's behaviour. Being excluded from school led to a determination by the young people to change their behaviour in order to succeed in the attainment of educational qualifications and hence prove their worth:

> I proved them wrong ... because they weren't expecting me to get one, and I got nine GCSEs ... so they were shocked. Even the teachers said to me 'well done', I was shocked ... I feel like I've challenged them.
> (Lucinda, 17, London)

Destinations and aspirations

Over a third of the interviewees moved to another school following their exclusion and two-thirds were in further education at the time of being interviewed (see Appendix 3). Almost half had gained some qualification at the time of being interviewed (see Appendix 4).

Some young people felt that they had a talent, which they did not want to waste. Hence, despite the lack of educational qualifications obtained at age 16 years (see Appendix 4), many sought to return to education or to gain permanent employment. In describing the driving force behind his decision to return to education, Anthony had said:

> I've got a brain up there right and I want to use it and I don't want it like wasting away.
> (Anthony, 18, Nottingham)

Commenting on the importance of completing education, Leon had poignantly said:

> I think no one should be excluded from school ... everyone deserves an education.
> (Leon, 16, London)

Some of the young people were aware of how difficult it was outside education. For example, after having talked about his plans to return to college and his music group, and his desire to succeed and have the 'bling-bling', Calvin had said:

> I would say stick in school, because there is nothing out there on the street.
> (Calvin, 16, Nottingham)

Factors involved in successful transitions

Social and cultural capital

The young African-Caribbean interviewees in this study mentioned several resources that provided the social and cultural capital to support them: family and friends, their local community, sympathetic teachers, social workers, agency workers and mentors, religious groups and alternative sites of education and schooling. These resources transcended gender and social class and whether they had one or two African-Caribbean parents or whether they had been raised in care.

The young people report that having the support and encouragement from family members and friends significantly enhances their route to a successful transition. The most positive and productive support included: practical advice and guidance; help with accessing information; emotional support and reassurance; a belief in the young person's account of events; and a shared sense of understanding the young person's experiences:

> I'm getting help from my teachers and school, my mum, grandparents, brother and sisters, friends and so on. They are all very supportive. They'll go onto the internet and find stuff like colleges, application forms or work placements and so they are supportive in that aspect.
> (Sirita, 16, London)

In addition to providing support, family members also acted as role models for the young people, demonstrating the realistic achievability of positive goals:

> I would say the person that made a lot of impact for me was my sister, going to university and living the lifestyle, going away. I admired that in certain ways ... I thought if she can do it, I can do this then ... I can't make her *[sister]* pass and then I fail ... because that's going to spoil the pattern ... so I had to keep the pattern going.
> (Roger, 15, London)

Friends were also an important source of support, as a shared sense of lifestyle, attitudes and experiences drew them into a group, which gave them a comforting sense of togetherness, especially if they too had experienced problems at school. They offered the excluded young person non-judgemental advice (but only when sought by the excludee themselves), sympathy, understanding and a means of escape from the exclusion label for the young person:

> ... they are just there, if I wanted to talk to them, I would talk to them.
> (Keenan, 18, Nottingham)

The social and cultural capital available to the young person was illustrated by Nelson who talked about the help he had been offered by members of his community:

> I just know they're there ... it's most of them from round here, they all ask me if I'm OK and help me ... they say to my mum 'if he wants this and that I can help'. It's nice really cos they're on my side.
> (Nelson, 16, London)

For some this was also available from their church community:

> … when I go to the church like, because there like the bishop knows like I told him what happened, they were praying for me like and like it feel like there's people that care like about me.
> (Lee, 16, London)

A small number of the excluded young people had mentioned that they had received support from sympathetic teachers from their excluding school. For example, Tamara had said:

> … she sent me work to do … she's one of the teachers that has always been there for me.
> (Tamara, 15, London)

However, despite all good intentions of the teacher, pressures from the excluding school had meant that such support was usually short-lived.

Some of the young people had been raised in care. This had meant that they had been allocated at least one social worker, who many saw as a substitute for a parental figure:

> … the social worker's like your parent basically.
> (Ray, 18, Nottingham)

These social workers had provided the young person with the emotional support and advice:

> I don't know, it just upset me when I had to leave *[care home]* … they all liked me. I don't know, I do miss them … they supported me really in everything. If I'd be upset she'd talk to me.
> (Rachael, 19, Nottingham)

Initiatives set up and run specifically by the black community, and designed to cater for the needs of young African-Caribbean people have also been beneficial to the positive self-identification of excludees and their successful transition into adulthood. This was the most popular type of support mentioned by these young people, with 28 referring to it:

> I just woke up one day and thought, what should I do? So I went to *[community organisation]*, I needed to speak to somebody. I feel like I needed to speak to someone. He *[agency worker]* goes 'Oh yes,

> whatever'. So I sorted it out, we met three different times. I spoke about everything. He was telling me about my relationship with my mother. Made me feel a lot better.
> (Bernard, 19, Nottingham)

And:

> … he *[mentor]* was like one of us, like the students … not the same age, but he knew what it was like.
> (Calvin, 16, Nottingham)

In emphasising the value of the community organisations, Sirita relayed the message she had taken away from the one that had helped her:

> … don't let no one put you down and just have supportive people around you.
> (Sirita, 16, London)

Access to resources and alternative provision

Many of the young people had aimed to pursue educational goals by finding more suitable alternatives to schooling. These included home tuition and enrolling on courses that the young people found more stimulating, such as music and drama courses. The young people had spent an enormous amount of time, energy and effort when on these courses, seeking not only to gain a qualification but also to develop it into a career:

> … at the end of this *[performing arts]* course I'm going to start going to the studio, to do my singing … I performed on the carnival stage and like someone spotted me from there, and said they wanted to manage me … I want to keep learning and learning, and at the moment I'm doing this course so I can get used to being on stage, for my confidence.
> (Latisha, 18, Nottingham)

Other studies have found that a significant factor in the shaping of the young person's transition is the availability and take-up of information and resources designed to help those excluded from school (Thomson *et al.*, 2003). In this study, the young people found that such resources were initially difficult to access. The primary reason given was not knowing where to start looking. All young people in the study had access to resources and used them to one degree or another. For the majority of those people, the access they had was from the non-statutory sector:

> ... *[the Director of the Community Empowerment Network (CEN)]* helped, he gave me comfort, yeah comfort and lots and lots of advice ... *[the Director of CEN]* is good, really good.
> (Lucinda, 17, London)

However, those living in care had found access to statutory help more readily available and commented on its value:

> ... the ISSP, they giving me help as well ... they like keeping me off the streets like ... like more constructive things to do like more positive things on my mind.
> (Leon, 16, London)

Similarly, on being referred to post-exclusion units and centres, young people had found an increase in their access to information and resources:

> I can go and talk to them whenever ... they just listen and give me advice and help, or say what I can do.
> (Leon, 16, London)

Class and economic capital

The economic capital available to the young people was an important determinant on the availability and take-up of resources. As expected, those from a more economically advantaged position (i.e. those of middle-class background) were much more able to draw on resources to aid transition. This is best illustrated by David whose parents immediately sought legal advice following the exclusion from school:

> ... cos he *[stepfather]* cared and wanted to help me out of the situation.
> (David, 17, Nottingham)

However, this was not possible for most of the interviewees. Their lack of access and availability to funds to assist reintegration into mainstream education and management of social exclusion was a recurring theme in the interviewees' accounts:

> I wouldn't be at college because at the end of the day I'm not going to college to find I didn't have any money to get there. I'd rather not go … No resources to go to college … She *[mother]* paid my auntie £30 a week to look after me. Out of that £30, I didn't get nothing for college … I'd say as soon as you're 16 grab it while you can because you know when you're 16 to 19 you've got every opportunity … grab all the courses. That's because at that stage you get a grant. When you are turning up on time you get a grant. But when you turn 19 it sort of stops.
> (Bernard, 19, Nottingham)

Focus, ambition and being determined to overcome the exclusion label

The educational ambitions of the young people excluded from school acted as an important factor in their transition pathway. Although they had very bad experiences of school and had been seriously let down by mainstream education, many still acknowledged the importance of education:

> … when I was at home *[after exclusion]* and I didn't have nothing to do, I was just thinking right I'm not going to get any GCSEs and so I can't get a job and stuff, so then I just started thinking and then while I was out of school I just done work at home and then when I got into a centre I just like knew everything I should have done, so I was good.
> (Miranda, 16, London)

They had sought to return to education to either retake GCSEs or go to college to study what they viewed as more interesting, stimulating and useful courses. For many of the young people, in particular the males, this was an interest in music. Talking about his NVQ in music technology and plans to study music at college, Earl had said:

> I want a career in music and I'm going to achieve it.
> (Earl, 18, Nottingham)

The young people's self-perception also acts as a significant factor in the success of their transitional pathways. The sense of injustice they felt drives their determination to overcome the exclusion label and to succeed. One way of doing this is by rejecting the stigmatising representations of themselves and developing more affirming representations of their community and culture, and hence a more positive version of self:

> I think in a way it's kind of opened my eyes a bit more ... like I've got to face problems in my life but sometimes it's not going to be an easy way for me to get out of it, I'll have to face it like head on and deal with it ... I suppose in a way it's kind of made me stronger like because I'm less afraid to put my opinions across and stronger in the way that I cried about it but now I don't think I would again.
> (Tamara, 15, London)

For some, a spiritual dimension was instrumental in increasing their self-awareness, self-respect and resilience:

> ... and God as well, because, at the same time I was going through that patch, I used to read the Bible a lot, my mum told me to read certain Psalms, she used to say before I go to school I read certain Psalms and when I come home I read it as well ... after that incident I made sure that it was done every single day I read the Bible ... it made me feel stronger, like, cos in the Bible that I read it's got certain titles like what it would be like if you're worried or angry and what to do with that certain mood. It makes you feel a lot better, so I'm like I can just do anything.
> (Lucinda, 17, London)

Summary

Even if they acknowledged that something they had done had led to their exclusion, the young people expressed an overwhelming sense of injustice, which was exacerbated by the belief that punishment was more severe for black pupils than it was for white pupils. Being excluded led to a loss of dignity, respect and self-worth. However, these responses are temporary, as many young people were determined to resist official expectation of them. They still found it a struggle to overcome the negative aspects of school exclusion and tended to see it as illustrative of their likely social exclusion in wider society and as an impediment to gaining meaningful employment. For some, it had led to involvement in criminal activities.

Many observed that exclusion acted as a 'critical moment' for them, making them reassess what they had been doing and refocus their energy, leading to a sense of maturity and attempts to gain control over the direction of their transition into adulthood. In spite of acknowledging the detrimental effects of exclusion, they still aspired to continue their education and had high levels of optimism of finding work.

Unanimously, the interviewees identified the availability of social and cultural capital as essential for surviving. Family, friends, community, sympathetic teachers, social workers, mentors, religious groups and alternative sites of education all combined to provide the resources for the majority of young people in the study to have made successful transitions.

3 The role of family members in transitions

Lucinda (London)

Lucinda is a 17-year-old young woman who had experienced two fixed-term and one permanent exclusion by the age of 13. The official reason for the exclusion is anger and violence. Lucinda strongly objects to being labelled as 'aggressive, intimidating, loose and wild', and says that teachers neglected her special educational needs because they saw her as a problem child. The support of family, friends, Saturday school and community projects enabled her to overcome the bad reputation she had gained at school. After two years of struggling, Lucinda recently returned to school, entering year 11. She is not enthusiastic about her new school and doubts that it will compensate for the education that she missed because she is not studying for GCSEs. Lucinda believes that overcoming school exclusion has given her the stamina, communication skills and independence to deal with difficult situations and ultimately to go to college. Her goal is to study computing or childcare. Stressing that her true potential is being ignored, Lucinda is trying harder.

Introduction

Although some of the young people had mentioned the significance of their friends in their transitions, they had primarily discussed the key roles played by family members. This chapter focuses on the role of the family in the young people's transitions. In doing so, it explores the significance of immediate and extended family members in the young person's management and further prevention of the exclusion label. Sixteen of the young people nominated a family member to be interviewed (see Appendix 5). For 13 of these this person was the mother, for one both mother and father were interviewed and the other two nominated a sister and grandfather.

Views about school, education and the young person before the exclusion

Before the exclusion, most family members had no expectation that anything would go wrong:

> ... everything was smooth and nice, he'd never been in any trouble.
> (Mother of 16-year-old Lee, London)

These views were usually reinforced by positive reports about the young person from the school:

> I always used to have good reports about her, she is quite bright.
> (Mother of 17-year-old Rose, Nottingham)

Although relatives outside the immediate family also expressed positive views about the young person's school before the exclusion incident, they had also had some cautionary feelings. For example, Richard's parents had expressed concern at the restrictions of the school curriculum:

> ... he is demotivated from the style of work they do. He's very good at art, yet he's failing in art at school because the system says draw this vase or whatever. He can't use his own creativity. A lot of black kids have so much creativity it is stifled in the school environment. Completely stifled.
> (Father of 18-year-old Richard, Nottingham)

Education is seen by black families as an important and valuable necessity (Mirza and Reay, 2000). It is not surprising therefore that young black people often find themselves immersed in a strong value system, which seeks to encourage them towards successful transitions via high educational attainment (Rhamie and Hallam, 2002). In the present study, the importance of education was often emphasised as a resource for struggling against racial bias:

> Keenan doesn't realise that education is a must ... as a black person in a white man's society, education is a must.
> (Mother of 18-year-old Keenan, Nottingham)

A state of educational limbo

While some of the young people and their families had been lucky enough to be able to quickly access support and resources allowing them to get onto community projects and Pupil Referral Units, many had been seriously let down by the statutory provision that is supposed to advise and guide the young people and their families through the exclusion process. Some young people had been left at home with nothing to do, suspended in uncertain territory while waiting for a decision about their education. For example, Ray's grandfather had said:

> ... they stopped at home for months, not go to school. For weeks they don't go to school.
> (Grandfather of 18-year-old Ray, Nottingham)

Being excluded at a key stage in their education (i.e. around GCSE stage), being given inadequate support from statutory provision and being faced with such an indeterminate state had devastating effects on the young people's transitional process:

> ... no support *[from the school]*. They *[school]* sent some stupid homework, which was not really adequate, was not revision. Then he missed out on all his revision.
> (Mother of 16-year-old Lee, Nottingham)

Views on education after the exclusion

After the exclusion and having gone through the experience of appeals and panel meetings, although the young people's families had continued to believe in the value of education, they had also developed negative views of the education process:

> ... the system has failed him, he's been demotivated completely.
> (Mother of 18-year-old Richard, Nottingham)

Such negative views were based partly on their feelings of having experienced racial discrimination:

> ... race does play a part because I just feel that the system, you know, that they fail the black children ... they're being ignored and the teachers have low expectations of them.
> (Mother of 17-year-old Lucinda, London)

Similarly, Earl's mother had said:

> ... the majority of these schools, I'm sure they don't want to educate black children ... I think it's racism. I really think so. The amount of black children I've heard have been excluded from school.
> (Mother of 18-year-old Earl, Nottingham)

Roger's mother had highlighted the class aspect in addition to the racial discrimination:

> ... the teaching and the teachers have a white middle-class view of the black child ... which is fuelled by the media, and I don't really think some of our kids stand a chance.
> (Mother of 15-year-old Roger, London)

It was felt that this type of discrimination was illustrative of practices in wider society:

> ... they *[black people]* can't get to the top because there is always people stopping them from getting up there ... It is still hard for the black youths of today, one because they can't get a job, two the police think because they are walking around in gangs right they are up to something ... it makes no difference what colour skin we are, we are all equal but we are not treated equally.
> (Mother of 17-year-old Rose, Nottingham)

The effects of the school exclusion

The exclusion of the young person from school has been found to also have serious detrimental effects on their families (Parsons *et al.*, 1996; Pomeroy, 2000). It is not surprising that all the families had reported that the exclusion had affected their relationships with the young person. For all, the exclusion was a difficult and stressful time. For a few, this put the relationship under strain:

> It was like she had PMT 24 hours a day. I'm telling you, you couldn't control her. She was out of control. It got to the point where I left home ... and left her in the house on her own and let her survive ... all I done was put electric in, gas and make sure she had food ... I even got reported to the council that I left her in the house ... basically it got to the point where I could not live with her.
> (Mother of 17-year-old Rose, Nottingham)

For a small minority of the young people's immediate family members, their relationships with other members of the extended family had temporarily broken down:

> They *[young person and siblings]* were fighting all the time. It got to the point where they were arguing and fighting, because of the problems and the situation ... it was unmanageable. Then she *[sibling]* left home. The other daughter, the eldest one, she left home as well and moved into a flat on her own.
> (Mother of 17-year-old Rose, Nottingham)

However, for the majority, the relationship between the young person and the family strengthened:

> ... it made us closer ... he was able to open up a lot more to me.
> (Mother of 15-year-old Gavin, London)

> I've always been close to my daughter, but it's brought me a bit more
> closer. We've got a tight bond, we've got a very tight bond.
> (Mother of 17-year-old Lucinda, London)

Many black families are keenly aware of a culture of respectability that exists both within the black community and wider society (Dove, 1998). To develop and maintain a respectable status, the black family is required to disprove negative ideas about being dysfunctional, disrespectful and pathological. There is a sense of shame attached to exclusion, particularly within their immediate community. For example, Richard's mother said:

> ... it is difficult to describe how embarrassed you feel. You get angry with
> the child as well, it's just nature, it's natural to say 'why, you know better'.
> (Mother of 18-year-old Richard, Nottingham)

Coping with the aftermath of the exclusion

The young people's families had reacted to being sidelined by mainstream education and the statutory provision by seeking to empower themselves. They did so by seeking help from voluntary community organisations, through the process of appeals against the exclusion and by demanding educational rights for the young people:

> I think *[Gavin]* felt he was on trial, but it was down to his mum and *[the
> Director of CEN]* to plead for his innocence because at the end of it we
> weren't gonna let *[Gavin]* down.
> (Mother of 15-year-old Gavin, London)

Like the young people, family members had viewed the exclusion as unfair. For example:

> ... it wasn't justified. At the end of the day it went through a court of law
> and he was found not guilty. What he was accused of he hadn't actually
> done ... *[but]* the *[school]* governors aren't going to side with the parents,
> they side with the headteacher.
> (Father of 18-year-old Richard, Nottingham)

Although these feelings of unfairness had angered family members and had been emotionally difficult for them, they had also been a key factor in their determination to clear the young person's name or help them overcome the exclusion:

> I found it a terrible, terrible, terrible time, I found the whole thing really, really traumatic … I don't know it was the initial shock of him being excluded to begin with … it was very traumatic for me, I was nervous, I felt very nervous at the time … but I knew on the outward I had to be strong, I had to go about the right channels and look at the different means to help him with the appeal, but on my quieter moments I felt within myself like a wreck.
> (Mother of 15-year-old Roger, London)

For many, additional stress was caused in families seeing the difficult time that the young person was experiencing:

> … coming up to five weeks or so when he was off school. I thought 'no, enough is enough' … I could see Earl getting depressed at home because all his sisters were getting up and going to school … I started going up to the school and sometimes one of the teachers would bring homework here for him and I'd have to take it back up to the school. It started to stress me out as well. I just didn't have Earl to look after. I had three other children at home as well. It started to get me down, stresses, watching him going through all that stress as well.
> (Mother of 18-year-old Earl, Nottingham)

For some people though, coping had not been such an emotionally difficult experience:

> … they *[appeal panel]* were very rude, they were unwelcoming as well, but I'm a strong-natured person, so I was able to cope with such people, you know, not be easily intimidated at all … I thought to myself, my daughter, she's a bright child, so I was more determined that no, I'm going to prove them wrong.
> (Mother of 17-year-old Lucinda, London)

As well as being driven by a need to help the young person's self-esteem by resisting the exclusion label, families had also found their emotional strength in their desire to overcome negative stereotypes about the black family and the black culture:

> … everyday I think, everyday I thought I couldn't deal with it … but I know I had to, Gavin was the one that kept me going because I could see the rapid deterioration in him … he weren't going to be another statistic because he's black and he's young, you know.
> (Mother of 15-year-old Gavin, London)

At times, perseverance was met with additional hostility and obstruction from the excluding school. This however, made the family member even more determined:

> I went up the school one morning … he *[headmaster]* saw me sitting there and I went at 8 o'clock in the morning. He was doing nothing, just standing up there. I saw him at 12 o'clock in the afternoon, he came out and he said to the receptionist 'tell Mrs Smith to make an appointment because I've got lots of things to do', so I turned round to him and said 'it's me who's Mrs Smith, so you can talk directly to me', he said 'oh, can you just make an appointment', so I said 'no, I'm waiting', I said 'it's my child, so I will wait' so he called me at 12 o'clock.
> (Mother of 16-year-old Lee, London)

Accepting the young person's interpretation

For many, a belief in the young person's version of events and the blood ties that existed between the families and the young person had been a strong driving force behind their determination not to give up:

> … because he's my child and I knew, with all my kids, they will tell me the truth … it *[belief]* gave me strength because I was saying 'I can't fail my son in this'.
> (Mother of 16-year-old Lee, London)

One of the reasons for believing the young person's version of events leading up to the exclusion was suspicion of the school's motives:

> … basically they said she was excluded because of her behaviour in the classroom or a fight or something I can't remember what it was … but it was a bit stupid, because there was more than one child involved and what happened was they went back to the school. Why wasn't she able to go back to school? It could have been because the teachers cannot

control her and she was probably too much for them, or because of her
colour, because she did get racial remarks from one of the teachers and I
went up to the school and asked why did the teacher call my daughter a
black so and so. And he goes 'oh it was just a slip of the tongue' and I
said 'I don't think it should be a slip of the tongue. It's a teacher, he is not
supposed to be abusive towards a child like that', so it could be because
of that as well.
(Mother of 17-year-old Rose, London)

Others, too, had been aware of racial discrimination in the exclusion of the young
person:

… she had a fight with a white girl, the white girl accused Lucinda of
stealing her mobile phone, which evidently she didn't. The white girl,
because she's white and she goes to one of the Catholic schools … the
teachers, you know, they're racist, I have to say it plainly, they treat the
black girls differently from how they treat the others … they excluded
Lucinda and not her … to be honest I just said to them 'well, you know I
believe my daughter, you believe your staff, I believe my child and the
reason why you do this is because she's a black child, not any other
reason' and that's me, I just come out frankly with my observation of the
situation.
(Mother of 17-year-old Lucinda, London)

Some believed that the young person was incapable of carrying out the sort of
behaviour that they had been accused of. For Anthony's mother in particular, this
belief was later confirmed when he was cleared of the teacher's accusation that he
had made a sexual comment to her:

… eventually they found out that she *[teacher]* lied and he had done three
months in prison and got put on the Sex Offenders' List for nothing.
(Mother of 18-year-old Anthony, Nottingham)

Some believed the young person because of the blood ties that existed between
them. This was particularly so for mothers who demonstrated their clear love for and
dedication to their child:

… nothing will crush my respect and my love for my children, nothing
would, nothing.
(Mother of 15-year-old Tamara, London)

However, such views about the importance of blood ties also came from extended family members. For example, Ray's grandfather had said:

> I love them. I love them. That's what I'm here for.
> (Grandfather of 18-year-old Ray, Nottingham)

Providing support

Practical support had been given by family members in a variety of ways. One way in which practical support was given was in terms of helping the excluded young person with learning and accessing and using resources:

> I came into the school and I sat with him in the library and we studied those extra subjects, ... and so I came in, and we did extra work. I went out and bought books, we went to the school library, you know ... they wanted to expel him, they wanted him out of the school, and I said no, so that was the compromise, and my boss allowed me to work particular shifts so that I could go to the school on particular days, whatever lessons, whatever periods they were. So that's what I did ... I mean, we had a good time because I learnt how funny my son was.
> (Mother of 17-year-old David, Nottingham)

Another way in which support was provided was by giving the young person advice:

> I just said whenever he feels that they are winding him up, just to sit down and count to ten, just try and ignore them.
> (Mother of 18-year-old Earl, Nottingham)

Parents' views of the schools are often influenced by their own past negative experiences of schooling (Wright *et al.*, 2000; Blair, 2001). These shared experiences help the family member understand and advise the excludee:

> ... like I said to him that there are two roads to take in life. I've done that road, you understand me? I've been down that bad road.
> (Mother of 18-year-old Keenan, Nottingham)

Such emotional support was underpinned by the families' desire to help the young person, not only with the exclusion, but also with the transitional process. This was particularly the case for matters relating to cultural identity. Here family members are seen as vital to culturally affirming the young person's identity and sense of self. Indeed, the role that Ray's grandfather had played in affirming Ray's cultural identity as a mixed-race individual, part Jamaican, was clearly significant in Ray's transitional process:

> ... our culture is different ... so you need someone from their own culture to talk to them.
> (Grandfather of 18-year-old Ray, Nottingham)

Sources of support

The majority of interviewees mentioned the need for practical advice about the exclusion process and other education options. Most sought to cope by becoming better educated about the exclusion process, their rights as parents and their children's rights. For those interviewees who had managed to access the information by themselves, it was felt that doing so had helped them cope much better:

> ... every human being has rights ... so I had to find out Tamara's rights in school, my rights as her parent, what I can do for her. So, once I knew those, I then know what route to go down.
> (Mother of 15-year-old Tamara, London)

However, for most of the families, support from others was required to cope with the exclusion and its aftermath. Family members had sought support from a variety of statutory and voluntary resources. Statutory resources included mentors that were attached to the school, social services and educational psychologists. For some, these statutory resources had been helpful:

> ... his social worker was a source of help. I don't know how he's been so lucky because she is still supporting him. I don't know how she does it and gets away with it. She has bent over backwards ... I owe her so much.
> (Mother of 18-year-old Anthony, Nottingham)

However, many had found the support from these statutory resources to be inadequate:

> I even went to Social Services and asked Social Services for help and I'd been there three times, 'come back the next day and we will sort

something out', so I went back, was there for a couple of hours giving us the run around … then they said 'she's your child, you have to look after her yourself'.
(Mother of 15-year-old Rose, Nottingham)

Similarly, the families reported a variety of experiences of the treatment given to them by the excluding school's teachers. For some of the families, teachers were helpful:

> … even when Earl was excluded, he *[teacher]* said to me that if I wanted he would come and give Earl extra tuition, for him to catch up with his work, which I thought was quite nice of him.
> (Mother of 18-year-old Earl, London)

Although it is the responsibility of the excluding school to send work home to the excluded young person or to make arrangements for the work to be collected, schools often fail to do so (Hayden and Dunne, 2001). This was found to be the case for many of the young people interviewed here. For example, although a few, such as Earl's mother (above), had reported teachers being helpful, for the majority, schoolteachers had been unhelpful and hostile:

> I had to be phoning them up to send homework and sometimes they didn't send any … I phoned the school all about this, you know, I've been up the school and can't get in touch with the teachers, I can't do this. I've phoned the school 'oh yes we'll send the papers', nothing is sent. So they reckon he'll fail anyway.
> (Mother of 16-year-old Lee, London)

On the other hand, the support from voluntary organisations had been viewed as particularly beneficial, not only with providing emotional support and advice for both the young person and the family member, but also in helping with appeal meetings:

> *[The Director of CEN]* was very good, very supportive … he went according to the DfES guidelines, he was very good, and he was able to point to certain points that they missed and things like that.
> (Mother of 17-year-old Lucinda, London)

Similarly, Tamara's mother had said:

> *[The Director of CEN]* would give me advice on what to do, and I'd do it … CEN is very helpful, you need an organisation like CEN … *[the*

> *Director of CEN]* has more experience and more knowledge, so it's not
> something I could have really done on my own.
> (Mother of 15-year-old Tamara, London)

Those voluntary groups that specialised in working with black families were viewed
as being of critical and valuable assistance, largely because they had a shared
sense of understanding of what the excluded young person and their family were
going through, and their experiences as black members of society:

> So I spoke to *[the Senior Community Development Officer]* and she got
> me in contact with OUR, which was part of the black family group who
> helps black parents or people who have mixed-raced children where they
> are having problems at school … OUR is more helpful towards black
> issues of parents and people who have got problems as well … OUR was
> supportive.
> (Mother of 17-year-old Rose, Nottingham)

The important role of the local church was also mentioned by some of the
interviewed families:

> … she's learning about black history there too.
> (Mother of 16-year-old Sirita, London)

Extended family members have also been found to be a valuable source of help,
assistance and guidance (Dove, 1998). For example, Roger's mother had said:

> … my parents helped, he *[young person]* has got extremely good and
> supportive grandparents.
> (Mother of 15-year-old Roger, London)

The available economic capital is also an important factor to the accessibility of
support and resources. Indeed, many of the family members interviewed had found
this to be the case. For some it even exacerbated the racial factor:

> … the bottom line of it and I've realised, it's not so much about being
> black you know, it's about being poor … I went into the schools, what
> support that they actually give the poor children in the bottom band, on
> the bottom set, bottom group, compared to what they give the top, middle
> to top children, they've prepared them for this, that … it's not necessarily
> about being black, but because you are black and you are poor, it's even
> worse. They have no hope for you.
> (Mother of 16-year-old Sirita, London)

Resisting the stereotypes

The educational system's pigeon-holing of black pupils as underachievers, problematic and unteachable has been well documented (Gillborn and Gipps, 1996; Ofsted, 1996; Mirza and Reay, 2000; Reay, 2000; Blair, 2001; Rhamie and Hallam, 2002). The majority of the families interviewed had felt that the young person had been labelled in this way. For example, in talking about the way in which she had thought the school and appeal panel had viewed her son, Gavin's mother had said:

> ... they *[appeal panel]* saw Gavin as a stereotypical black youth, because he's very dark, he doesn't smile a lot, he can look very intimidating because of his colour and I just think they put him into a category before they even saw him ... I do believe it is a race issue and I think when you're dealing with black youths and families they know nothing about our culture, they know nothing about us at all.
> (Mother of 15-year-old Gavin, London)

Some also felt that they had been stereotyped in the same way:

> ... they *[school]* said of me that I was a dysfunctional, abusive parent.
> (Mother of 16-year-old Sirita, London)

They then had to defend themselves as members of the black community and symbols of black culture in situations where they felt they were under attack, such as in panel meetings:

> It's another thing when you go to school they always expect the black parents to go on badly ... I never gave them that satisfaction, not once.
> (Mother of 14-year-old Yolan, London)

Many of the families felt that the value and importance of the black extended family unit needed to be appreciated more as a site of struggle against discrimination and oppression. As such, greater encouragement and support, as opposed to condemnation, needs to be given to black families:

> ... we *[black families]* need to come together and share ideas and experiences ... that's how we learn and that's how we can get help and sort out our kids.
> (Mother of 17-year-old Lucinda, London)

The families also commented that positive black role models needed to be found in society:

> Because all the black teachers in this school, like, they don't motivate the black children, to say 'oh this is your history, you can do this or that', whatever, like they have to prove something to the white teacher that they're not on the black children's side and this is the problem. They *[children]* have nobody to face as a role model who is like them.
> (Mother of 16-year-old Lee, London)

In talking specifically about the help and support that the young people and their families had received from voluntary organisations that specialised in working with black people, it was said:

> I think that it is good, you know the black groups helping black people, and you find as well that there are some people who don't know about these organisations and what is going on, and also people who have got mixed-race kids as well they don't know where they can go for help. Because they are probably not getting help from school. We need more black teachers, we need more black politicians who are going to help and more black organisations.
> (Mother of 17-year-old Rose, Nottingham)

Summary

This chapter examined the experiences of and the effects on the family of the excludees. Family members were generally optimistic about education before the exclusion, so were devastated when the young person was left without any schooling provision at all. After exclusion, families still believed in the value of education but had negative views of the education system. The exclusion had a huge impact on the families and they coped with its aftermath by adopting an attitude of determination, and helped the young person to cope by being accepting and giving support. They referred to several external sources where they had been able to obtain support, advice and practical help. In spite of this, many believed they and their children had been negatively stereotyped, and felt keenly the importance of replacing the damaged image of black families and black culture by a more accurate and positive representation.

4 Social capital, community organisations, social networks and transitions

Sirita (16), London

Sirita was excluded at age 14 for allegedly hitting a teacher. The Community Empowerment Network (CEN) was integral to helping win her appeal. Her family and friends encouraged her to deal with the upsetting experience. Sirita maintains that her family listening to, believing and caring for her keeps her focused on success. She enjoys school less now because she is weary of teachers making accusations about her disrupting lessons. She is highly critical of the stereotypes that she believes are held by white teachers of black pupils as failing and violent.

Sirita believes that coping with school exclusion has greatly contributed to strengthening her character. As a result, she believes that she is now more mature, determined and aware. She has learnt how to deal with painful problems because she developed confidence and communication skills during the appeal procedures. Sirita argues that she has the will-power to work hard and get good grades in her GCSEs. She plans to go to beauty college and own a beauty salon, and is optimistic that her future aims will disprove the predictions of her teachers.

Introduction

While many of the young people mentioned family or friends as sources of support, nearly everyone, family members included, mentioned the importance of voluntary organisations.[1]

There were 15 community-based agencies and organisations across London and Nottingham mentioned by interviewees (see Appendix 6). In addition to having identified helpful organisations, the young people and their families had also highlighted particular individuals within the organisations who had played a key role in assisting them to overcome the exclusion. Although working as practitioners for voluntary and community organisations, these individuals represented unique and creative ways of working with the excludees and their families, which embodied a sense of social responsibility. This is because they have not only the in-depth knowledge about this area but also, in many cases, relevant first-hand experience. The representatives who were interviewed outlined the methods that these organisations used in working with the young people and their families, and how they empowered the young people and assisted them with their positive identity formation and reintegration into education and society. In particular, there is an emphasis on how some of these agencies were providing a service that they were not resourced to provide. They had felt a necessity to respond to an unmet need in the black community.

Community Empowerment Network (CEN)

CEN, based in London, was established in 2000 with a grant from the National Lottery Charities Board in order to provide advice, counselling, support, representation and training for people experiencing mistreatment and disadvantage in education, especially exclusion from school. CEN intervenes on a partnership basis in support of students and their parents experiencing problems with institutions, local education authorities and the Department of Education and Skills. CEN offers advice and assistance to promote genuine home–school partnership to secure conditions for the best kind of teaching and learning, and to support people challenging bullying and harassment. As a registered charity, CEN relies on donations.

Take-one Music Studio

Established in 1999, Take-one comprises a group of people who previously undertook their work under the umbrella of a community-based organisation. The staff at Take-one are a core group of young, committed, talented individuals who all share a passionate interest in music. The studio's primary aim is to provide a realistic environment and training for young, gifted artists and prepare them for careers within the music industry. It also aims to provide young people with alternative means of expressing themselves and to create a safe haven. As a result, it has grown into a drop-in facility for some excluded young people. It is funded through various short-term grants.

Positive Action Training and Recruitment Agency (PATRA)

PATRA East Midlands was established in 1987. It is a voluntary organisation with charitable status covering the areas of Nottingham, Derby and Leicester, and plays an integral part in effecting changes in attitudes, styles and traditional employment practices. Its aim is not merely to improve minority ethnic employment statistically but more importantly to effect a change in culture

continued

whereby it becomes normal and acceptable to see black people in all positions in employing organisations. Although PATRA's original remit did not cover dealing with school excludees, the Chief Executive found that it had to be reorganised in order to assist young people who had been excluded from school. This is because PATRA found, in looking at the under-representation of black people in employment, that many young black people were coming from backgrounds where they had experienced serious school difficulties, i.e. exclusion. For young people who are excluded from school, PATRA offers a mentoring programme that provides support and guidance. It receives revenue funds from various sources, which vary from year to year. However, 70 per cent of its total funding comes from the employers who take on trainees and fund trainees' allowances and training programmes.

Although the agencies varied considerably in their remit, they were all very similar in the type of support they offered to black young people who had been excluded from school. This included practical help such as providing alternative learning sites, advocacy and representation, assistance with reintegration into mainstream education, careers advice and employment guidance, as well as emotional support to improve family relationships and help the development of a positive identity.

The effects of the school exclusion

Because of their knowledge and experience, the organisations and workers recognised the immediate impact of the school exclusion was to make the young person feel alone:

> ... the big problem with exclusions is of course, by its very nature, by the way it works, you're made to feel that you are alone and an isolated case, there's nobody else like you.
> (Director, CEN, London)

For some, this isolation could result in more extensive feelings of exclusion:

> They don't feel part of that community. They're not recognised in that community. They are looked on as the thorn in the side in the community. You need to embrace these young people to become the next generation of young people that are going to be mothers and fathers of tomorrow.
> (Youth Advocate Manager, ISSP, Nottingham)

The experience of exclusion had also impinged on the young people and their families' self-worth and identity development:

> ... what we observed was, in more cases than not, they'd been damaged academically. Their esteem had gone. Their confidence had gone. They didn't think they could achieve any more once they were excluded ... so the ambition had gone, or had been taken from them if they were permanently excluded.
> (Senior Youth Worker, Team Libra, Nottingham)

They also observed the state of 'educational limbo' reported by the parents:

> ... many of those people excluded from school have been excluded from school a number of months, in some cases out of school a year or even maybe 18 months. They have many hours on their hands and they offend with other young people ... so you have a lot of these young people at the time that no one has given them direction to do nothing.
> (Youth Advocate Manager, ISSP, Nottingham)

The Senior Youth Worker for Team Libra (Nottingham) had also talked about the links between exclusion and crime:

> I think there is a link between exclusion, crime and drugs. Obviously once those students, their confidence has gone, their esteem has gone and they are not motivated any more so what are the options for them? They get into drugs ... they have low self-esteem. Lacked motivation, lacked pride, lacked desire, lacked forward movement to get into college or to get a job. It was easier to run around the streets, perhaps sell drugs.
> (Senior Youth Worker, Team Libra, Nottingham)

Being excluded had also, for the young people in particular, been perceived as an alarming realisation of the racist and discriminatory processes that they are likely to experience in wider society:

> ... racism is within the education system, it's within the housing system, it's within the job market, it's everywhere. What I'm saying is that for these young people ... is the recognition and ability to sort of logically think through this and things are just starting to drop into place. So these things could have been happening to them earlier, but, because they were more childlike, because they were more innocent if I can put it that way, maybe it didn't affect them so much. So for me part of the drop in

their achievements and attainments is the fact that they are also
beginning to feel the extra burdens of racism.
(Team Manager, Team Libra, Nottingham)

Providing help that was unavailable elsewhere

The work undertaken by the organisations was viewed by its workers as a response
to a discriminatory education system:

> The fact of the matter is the schools try and locate the problem, either
> inherently in the child because you can't do this or you can't do that, or
> you don't want to do this or that, or in the family, single-parent family ... if
> you're black and a single-parent family. There's something really wrong
> altogether. And it's the stereotyping, it's learning only prejudice and bias
> and myth from history.
> (Director, CEN, London)

It was also seen as a response to the vacuum created by the shortcomings of
statutory service provision and the lack of support they provided for young people
and families:

> Sometimes they phone you late at night because that's the time when
> they've managed to screw up enough courage to do so ... what's
> happening in the mainstream, what's happening in the schools, what's
> happening in the local authority, because I find sometimes that the
> response that they get *[from them]* is quite arrogant, you know 'how dare
> you bother me, don't you know I'm busy?' whereas my response is 'we're
> never too busy'.
> (Director, CEN, London)

Team Libra's (Nottingham) Team Manager had similarly highlighted the types of
negative responses that parents of excluded children reported:

> ... parents will actually contact us and say 'I've had this letter from the
> school, I don't really understand what it's all about, I've tried to talk to the
> school, the school are just accusing me of being stroppy, obnoxious, sort
> of like blocking the way of progress and that's not really the case. Will you
> come down and support us in this thing?'
> (Team Manager, Team Libra, Nottingham)

Indeed, for some workers, such discriminatory treatment and gaps in provision caused additional anger because it was viewed as a 'conspiracy' against the whole black community:

> ... all we want is quality of life. I don't believe black people should do it for free. We done it free in the early days, slavery. Ain't doing shit for free.
> (Youth Advocate Manager, ISSP, London)

Shared experiences

In addition to their training and knowledge, all the workers within organisations felt they understood the excludees' experience, in some cases because they themselves had been excluded:

> It's kind of weird because Take-one came about from my kind of travels through getting back on the straight and narrow, are you with me? Cos, I was like unemployed and not at school, and left with no qualifications and all that type of stuff. So, basically, I started off in my music career.
> (Manager, Take-one, Nottingham)

Hence, their work was driven by genuine passion, a desire to assist and support the young people and their families, and a need to empower them as members of the black community:

> I have a commitment to the work and desire to do it. I enjoy doing what I'm doing. the reason I enjoy doing what I'm doing is because it is about young black men, and young black women as well.
> (Youth Advocate Manager, ISSP, London)

The extent to which the workers felt such desire and dedication in assisting the young people was illustrated by the time that they spent working, often on a voluntary basis, on the exclusion cases:

> ... from say 9 o'clock in the morning until 10 to 11 o'clock at night. And that's five, six, seven days a week.
> (Youth Advocate Manager, ISSP, London)

Another indicator of dedication was their claimed success rates:

> CEN has a 100 per cent success rate in terms of reintegration, either at the excluding school or the new school where the young person finds admission.
> (Director, CEN, London)

Indeed, some young people who had been successfully helped by the organisation in the past were returning with their shared experience and applying to assist the current intake of young people:

> … the organisation has aged, in that we're seeing mentees becoming mentors, which is great. You get a call out of the blue, somebody saying 'I was helped by Build ten or 11 years ago and I'm now employed or studying at university and I'd like to give something back.' So we have had an impact.
> (Chief Executive, Build, Nottingham)

However, workers were keen to emphasise that having a sense of shared experience with the young people did not mean that they were not fair or rigorous in dealing with cases:

> The other thing is that we are not in any way sloppy about what we do. We're very rigorous in interrogating the situation, we want to know what happened and we want to know why is it escalated to this point, what did you do that escalated it or what could you have done that would have defused the situation?
> (Director, CEN, London)

Working for the empowerment of black individuals and successfully assisting the young people overcome their exclusion clearly gave the workers job satisfaction:

> I would say too right, it is the most fulfilling, satisfying, challenging job I've done up to now, simply because I'm allowed to create something that's allowed to be innovative … I make contacts with all those relevant agencies but pull the strengths together with my support team to be able to support those young people.
> (Youth Advocate Manager, ISSP, London)

The community as an important learning site

There is an emerging body of research on community organisations as alternative 'learning sites' (Craig, 2002; DfES, 2003c). Studies indicate that black young people experiencing difficulties at school have often benefited greatly from learning out of school hours in community-run initiatives such as supplementary schools, mentoring projects and music-based projects (DfES, 2003c).

The Chief Executive of PATRA, Nottingham, explained:

> ... some of the children, because of their experiences within the classroom, do not want to go back into the school.
> (Chief Executive, PATRA, Nottingham)

The Development Worker from Black Families in Education Group, Nottingham had expanded on the reasons for this:

> *[Excludees]* feel that the education system has let them down ... a lot of children think 'my education has finished, what's the next move?'.
> (Development Worker, Black Families in Education Group, Nottingham)

Following exclusion, many black young people had severe misgivings about returning to the school environment and it was felt that community-based provision often played a vital role in re-engaging the young people in the educational process:

> ... a lot of young people, because of their experience through instilled racism, are more comfortable in working with people from their own kind, within organisations that provide that service.
> (Chief Executive, PATRA, Nottingham)

For the interviewed workers and their organisations, the community appeared to offer an alternative learning site. This was provided in several ways. For some, it had offered supplementary schooling. In particular, such schooling focused on African-Caribbean history and culture:

> So for instance *[name of club]*, which is an after-school study club, was started by workers from Team Libra. It's an independent entity but it deals with working with young people, teaching them skills like Swahili, French and giving them African history in particular. So they get to learn a little bit about their background and they understand that the African person does have a fulfilled sort of history within the overall aims of what this civilisation is. We also work with other groups to try and develop things ...

> We sort of like work in a wide area of schools under black African-
> Caribbean specified issues.
> (Team Manager, Team Libra, Nottingham)

Indeed, one worker had commented on the importance of assisting young African-Caribbeans in this way:

> ... because it's something that they want to do, they are actually quite
> focused.
> (Youth Worker, Team Libra, Nottingham)

Similarly, another worker had explained the reasons for this:

> ... some boys couldn't wait to get out of school. They couldn't wait to go
> on an apprenticeship. They couldn't wait to be treated with a bit of
> respect, like young people. You know at college the lecturers show the
> students respect straightaway.
> (Senior Youth Worker, Team Libra, Nottingham)

Such support also helped to redress the perceived racist type of education that was largely being taught in mainstream education:

> ... it still is a monocultural education system, which is excluding some
> people.
> (Team Manager, Team Libra, Nottingham)

On the same note, one worker had discussed how and why black communities had specifically helped redress this racism:

> I think whát the black communities are looking for is change,
> transformation, new opportunities because people share a vision and that
> is most important. What's our vision? You know legacies of loss, and what
> I've been trying to work out is what is it that our young people remember,
> sometimes vaguely, because I feel that the problem with formal education
> very often is it destroys your rootedness and your sense of belonging to
> your family, relationship with parents and siblings as well as a relationship
> history.
> (Director, CEN, London)

Other types of alternative learning included more creative programmes, workshops and training courses that were designed around the young people's interests, for example, music, dance and drama:

> ... we also do other initiatives, which is like accreditation courses for
> young people, which is like the ... weightlifting qualification, the pool
> lifeguard qualification, first-aid qualifications. We are also working on
> accreditation on music workshop, issues you know young people express
> interest in music. We have initiatives we are doing, barbering
> accreditation ... hair and beauty ... basically what we try and do really is
> just kind of look on what would be the norm for young people in an
> education context ... what they view they would like to achieve and how
> do we qualify them to turn the system, to be able to get on.
> (Youth Advocate Manager, ISSP, London)

These special-interest programmes were designed not only to provide the young
people with their own space and to stimulate them, but also to give them 'that push
start' (Youth Worker, Team Libra, Nottingham) by enabling them to use their interests
and skills to enhance their future prospects:

> ... the community studio is primarily like a drop-in space but it's there to
> use music as a tool, to develop young people's capacity to learn, to
> become professionals in their own right, to become leaders, to take
> responsibility.
> (Community Development Officer, Take-one, Nottingham)

In addition to these roles, the organisations provided the young people with 'life
education', in particular education about issues with which young black people are
stereotypically associated, i.e. drugs, sexuality, sexual health and teenage
parenthood:

> Quite often it's mainly young males we are dealing with so we talk about
> issues around teenage pregnancy and the responsibilities that they as
> males should have to their partners, to their children if they go down that
> road ... Also we do work around areas of sexual health and everything
> with young women as well, when it's necessary. Because it's not just a
> single-sex activity. We do quite a lot of work around drugs because our
> community is often given the title of the people that are, if you like,
> supplying the drugs to the whole of this country. I mean the fact that the
> country itself seems to be a drug-consuming nation is beyond me. It's not
> as if black people suddenly came into this country and started giving
> these things out left, right and centre.
> (Team Manager, Team Libra, Nottingham)

Methods of working with young people and their families

A variety of methods for working with the young people and their families had been adopted by the organisations and workers. These had depended on whether the organisation was an advocacy, mentoring or support group, for example. However, all the organisations had in their approaches provided a service that was based on mutual trust, respect and responsibility:

> … young West Indian black kids excluded from school and all that type of stuff that they say, they was all coming down here because of the music and the studio. And I allowed them to have an input and showed them a level of respect and trust that they just basically felt comfortable with.
> (Manager, Take-one, Nottingham)

Similarly, one worker had emphasised the fairness of such an approach:

> … we don't want to wrap our young black people up in cotton wool. When a young black person comes through our door and says 'I've been excluded' and this and that, we'll say 'OK. How might you have contributed to this?'
> (Chief Executive, Build, Nottingham)

The workers found that such respect, trust and encouragement had positive effects:

> Once they realise that someone actually believes what they say and can see where they are being chastised unfairly, a lot of them do calm down and their anger goes. They turn into quite good people.
> (Senior Community Development Officer, Black Families in Education Group, Nottingham)

This had meant that the workers were able to communicate with the young people in a way that was open, honest and supportive. Similarly, although the young people often looked up to the workers, the relationship between the worker and the young person was often viewed as an equal one:

> I know I've got a positive impact because, when I see them on the street, they are like 'oh are you all right?' … I'll ask them if they've done the lyrics for the track that they are supposed to be coming down to. I'll ask them if they are still playing football or things like that. Because I've done quite a lot of work with them, I know what kind of things they are into and it's just nice to see them out. When they see me it's like 'oh there's *[Youth*

Worker's name]. It just puts a smile on my face … they know I'm easy to talk to. I mess about with them. I bully them a little, nice bullying, well I'm like 'you come here, what are you doing?' They are all right with me. It's nice.
(Youth Worker, Team Libra, Nottingham)

In enabling the young people to replace the threatening images held of them (Sewell, 1997), the organisations had encouraged them to take an active role:

… we've been asked to try and reduce offending by 5 per cent … we go about that by young people attending what we call 'life skills sessions' but we are calling the shots … which is young people turning up on Thursday afternoons as part of the skills of addressing offending behaviour and we do like workshops, we'll bring in visitors, we'll bring in guest speakers to try and actually address empowerment with those young people, and it's very powerful stuff because the young people are able to talk about where they are in their lives, why they offend, what do they get out of offending, what kind of factors have gone on in their family background, the education, why they feel they are not getting a fair education … by doing so, we don't actually talk at the young people, we get the young people to contribute.
(Youth Advocate Manager, ISSP, London)

The workers had also encouraged changes in the young people's behaviour:

… we try and keep their minds occupied so, when they do get back into school, they've got something to look forward to when they come out of school and they can go to youth clubs and things like that. We've tried to also help them with the alternative provision, direct them in the right place.
(Youth Worker, Team Libra, Nottingham)

The workers also encouraged the young people to improve their relationships with others, especially with authority figures:

We will actually then run a series of things where we will look at things like relationships of the young people. So the relations that we will explore with the young people are relationships between them and their parents. Relationships between them and perceived authority figures, like teachers or the police or anything else. Relationships between the young people and their peers, because we often have this sort of area where

some young people are doing things just to impress their peers and that
can lead on to other things.
(Team Manager, Team Libra, Nottingham)

Improving and utilising family relations

The detrimental effects caused by exclusion from a school also extend to the
excludee's family (Cohen and Hughes, 1994, quoted in Parsons, 1999; Parsons *et
al.*, 1996; Pomeroy, 2000). In talking about such damaging effects, in particular the
feelings of powerlessness that many parents of excluded children often report, the
Senior Community Development Officer of Black Families in Education Group,
Nottingham, had said:

> We work from a parent's perspective: where the parent feels in control of
> their own child. Because they will go to one meeting and Social Services
> tell them, we are working with the child that way, the police are doing it this
> way, schools doing it another way. But the parent had no say in the whole
> process. Just feel they are being carried along. So we decided to get
> something together where the parents have to be consulted and they have
> a right to say, 'this is how I want to participate with my child in whatever
> your organisations are doing'. Just to give parents back some control.
> (Senior Community Development Officer, Black Families in Education
> Group, Nottingham)

The excludee's family has largely been found to be a valuable support network in
helping young people to overcome their exclusion (Pomeroy, 2000). The interviewed
workers had recognised the important role that family members played in supporting
their children with the exclusion process:

> … because parents like to support each other in the community, they talk
> to each other and people tell them about what resources are available for
> them … so they can support their child.
> (Development Worker, Black Families in Education Group, Nottingham)

Many of the organisations, especially the Black Families in Education Group, had
sought to empower and inform parents:

> It's about building parents as well. You need to give them awareness.
> Most people have two or three children. So if the eldest child is having
> problems at some point the younger one may experience. Just the fact

they have the same family name, going through the same school. So if you can empower that parent to deal with the situation they can protect the second child and the third child ... so we look at the situation and try to encourage parents.
(Senior Community Development Officer, Black Families in Education Group, Nottingham)

Enabling empowerment and assisting positive identity formation

The young people, their parents and the workers had all appeared to be aware of the racist and discriminatory stereotypes held by teachers, and the damaging effects of these stereotypes on the young person's confidence, self-awareness, identity development and opportunity of a fair education:

> ... educationwise teachers need to be alert and, 'trained' is the wrong word, they need to know that different cultures mean that different people will behave differently. Just because a young black child may express himself with his hands or may be coming from a different culture totally doesn't mean that he's going to be aggressive.
> (Senior Co-ordinator, Build, Nottingham)

A large part of assisting the young people and their families to overcome the exclusion was through empowerment. The workers did this by attempting to provide the opportunities denied to them by mainstream education:

> I just have a team that is trying to support the young people because of what they were supposed to get and have been denied, and try to do the best we can do within the parameters and move the boundaries and knock the door hard and move the doors off the hinges to make changes.
> (Youth Advocate Manager, ISSP, London)

Empowerment was also attempted via increasing the confidence and self-esteem of the young people:

> I think that most of the work we do is really around boosting their confidence and self-esteem.
> (Chief Executive, Build, Nottingham)

Coping strategies were also seen as an important part of empowerment:

> We found it really frustrating because a lot of what we found in the work we did in terms of exclusions was that black boys were experiencing a lot of racism in school and, as we all know, racism does exist in schools. And I think one particular part of our role was to help them channel issues of aggression, frustration into something positive. So, for example, we would ask them to make notes and when things happened we'd get them to write it down … control the pressure at times if you like.
> (Senior Youth Worker, Team Libra, Nottingham)

Empowering the young people and their families in this way was seen as having positive effects on their self-esteem and identity development. For example, the Senior Co-ordinator at Build, Nottingham had said about Calvin:

> Now, I mean Calvin *[has]* been through a lot, with the deaths of some young people that he knew and in his family. In Nottingham, major deaths like *[name of friend]* was a good friend of Calvin … Then the death of *[his brother]* as well. He's been through a lot … but I've seen him grow from a boy to a man to be honest in those two years, physically and mentally, he's become much taller and mentally he can communicate better with people.
> (Senior Co-ordinator, Build, Nottingham)

Reintegration into education and enhancing employability

All the workers had recognised the problem of reintegration difficulties for black excludees, especially for those who also have offended:

> The difference is that when people see your black skin to begin with you are already being marked down, if you like. What then happens is that, unfortunately, I'll go back to the thing with the identity cards, we already have systems in this country that penalise black people. We know that, there's no two ways about it. The problem we've got is that if a black person has a criminal record as well that further disadvantages them.
> (Team Manager, Team Libra, Nottingham)

As such, they had all sought to reintegrate the young person into mainstream education and enhance their employability status. They had done so not only by providing information, advice and support for the young people, but also by actually training them and equipping them with employable skills:

> ... the support that we have, good contact with different bodies to support those young people beyond being excluded from the school process, but being able to skill and train them, so that they can become employable. (Youth Advocate Manager, ISSP, London)

Many of the organisations had also provided the young people with contacts. For example, PATRA organised conferences in which the young people could learn about the education and employment options available to them.

Summary

There is a long tradition of community-led initiatives in supporting the transitional experience of young black people. Interviews with representatives of such initiatives, including one statutory organisation, revealed that they were seen as significant and fundamental in helping the excludees overcome the exclusion and make successful transitions into adulthood. This was achieved in a variety of ways, which included recognising immediate and longer-term effects of school exclusion, sharing understandings of the exclusion experience, providing alternative learning sites and assisting in improving family relationships, positive identity formation and reintegration into mainstream education. Essentially, these initiatives can be seen as responding in unique ways to a system that labels black people as underachievers and as having anti-education attitudes. They can also be seen as providing an important service, which they are not resourced to do, but feel they have to fulfil in order to respond to an unmet need.

5 Key issues and policy recommendations

Introduction

It is now widely recognised that the transition towards independent adulthood is more uncertain than it was. While many young people manage to successfully navigate this increasingly uncertain and complicated course, some experience significant difficulty along the way. The primary aim in undertaking the research was to examine the impact of school exclusion on transitions to adulthood. Government policies (e.g. SEU, 1999) have recognised that exclusion from school exacerbates and intensifies social exclusion. The focus of this study on the experiences of excluded young people is therefore highly relevant. Adapting Kelly and Kenway's (2001) assessment of the division between dynamic networks of youth transitions that connect family, schooling and employment, the study focused on the strategies these young people had adopted. An additional aim of the study was to provide much needed research evidence on which to base interventions to break the link between school exclusion and social exclusion for African-Caribbean communities. For this reason, after reflecting on the methods the study employed, it is worth reiterating the main findings that emerged and outlining their implications for policy formulation. The findings are summarised in relation to, first, exclusion, reintegration and transition and, second, support, networks and resourcing. In a broader sense, however, the messages emanating from the research are of importance for all areas of work with young people at risk of social exclusion and provide insights into how social inclusion and exclusion are reproduced.

Reflection on the methods employed in the study

This was a large study in terms of its depth. Thirty-three young people contributed and material was collected through over 100 interviews. The young people varied in their social situations and came from two areas that were characterised by different service provision. Information was collected from a variety of agencies: most were voluntary or charitable, some were solely for the black community but none was specifically set up to deal with school exclusion. The sample was limited in that all the young people who took part were contacted through agencies providing them with support. There are many young people with no such support and the prospects for them are unlikely to be as positive as those for the young people we interviewed.

Given that our focus was on the strategies that enable young people to make successful transitions following school exclusion, this bias was inevitable. However, although this bias leads us to give prominence to the role of the agencies, interviewees did reveal other, more individual, methods of coping with transition.

An additional strength of the study was the collection of material from different sources using the young person as the starting point and asking them to nominate other people we should interview. During pilot work, we were prepared for greater involvement of peers. However, although some young people were accompanied by friends during interviews, these friends rarely contributed to the material collected.

Similarly, during pilot work, we had introduced the procedure of giving the young people cameras with which to take pictures that could be used as a starting point for the second interview. This option was taken up by only a small proportion of the participants, with one bringing along an album containing pictures she had collected prior to the study. For most participants, no such prompt was required to facilitate the interviews and it must be concluded that a certain degree of flexibility in approach is needed in these types of studies to facilitate the participation of a range of people, especially those who are normally difficult to reach.

Exclusion, reintegration and transitions

The study found that, for this group of young people, there are many parts of their life on which school exclusion has an impact. These include their family, being left in 'educational limbo', involvement in crime and their transition to adulthood.

Impact on the young person and the family

The study found that school exclusion had a profound effect on both the young person and their family. The young people's reports of their experiences varied. However, a recurring theme throughout their narratives in this study is the sense of injustice they felt about the way they were excluded. This sense of injustice was reported as stemming from three sources. First, it followed from not having been allowed to put their case. It also arose from a feeling that they were labelled and stereotyped to the extent that teachers were effecting outcomes that they themselves had anticipated as inevitable. Lastly, it followed from the experience of seeing their white peers who were involved in the same or similar incidents being allowed to stay in school or return after a fixed term of exclusion while they were kept out of school or permanently excluded. The young people felt that exclusion greatly affected their performance and achievements. They believed that the stigmatising representations associated with exclusions had a very destructive effect on their schooling and beyond, and that the experience had damaged their esteem, sense of identity and future opportunities. However, for the majority of young people, these expressed disadvantages were short-lived and the support of family, friends and community agencies allowed them to reject the stigmatising representations of themselves and develop more affirming ones.

Fortunately, most of the young people were back in mainstream education, in employment or about to return at the time we contacted them and were optimistic about their lives and future, despite having experienced a difficult and disrupted education.

Parents and carers also felt that the exclusion was unjust, often echoing what their child felt. Parents and carers often disputed the reasons given by schools either because they felt that the situation had been overstated or they did not agree that the circumstances were as described. They reported the devastating effects on the well-being of the family and the confusion and the anger engendered by the whole situation. They felt stigmatised by their child's involvement in the school exclusion process. The critical issue here is how parents and families then dealt with that reality. Most felt obligated to support their child and give self-confidence, motivation and resilience to overcome the exclusion. Further, parents of many of the young people in the study were also products of the same schooling system. As some of them observed, they had to learn hard lessons at the interface with schools in the same way that their children are now doing. Their experience did not automatically lead them to make assumptions about the school environment as safe, valuing of all, respecting of all, supportive and in *loco parentis* (in *loco parentis* is interpreted mainly as schools being responsible for children's safety and discharging a duty of care towards them once parents have handed them over to their charge).

Being left in 'educational limbo'

For most young people excluded from school, the immediate support must focus on minimising the disruption in their education and social relationship (e.g. see German, 2001). Only 15 per cent of permanently excluded young people ever reintegrate into mainstream school (DfEE, 2000a). In the study, it was found that there was considerable variability in an immediate educational alternative being provided. For example, some young people were sent to a Pupil Referral Unit, but most were left without any immediate educational provision. Two consequences of this situation were that young people missed taking GCSE exams and that delays made it difficult for them to reintegrate into another school. In these instances, it was found that the support and resources received from family and community agencies were vital in re-engaging the young people in education. The challenge facing the Government is to ensure that there is continuity of access to education and opportunities to make up for lost schooling in the provision made for young black people excluded from school, particularly given their over-representation in the exclusion figures.

Involvement in crime

The recent Youth Survey conducted by the Youth Justice Board (2003) indicates that attachment to school protects young people from involvement in criminal activity. This is especially the case for boys from 12 to 16 years old. Success in school is an even stronger protective aspect. Some young people in the study reported their involvement in offending activities that coincided with being excluded from school. However, these young people also reported that they stopped offending when they became engaged in education or employment.

Transition to adulthood

As reported above, many young people obtained employment, some returned to education and a few engaged in neither of these. These findings highlighted the significance of the cultural and economic capital of family of origin in reproducing or overcoming disadvantage, or in facilitating the inclusion and advancement of young people excluded from school. Some parents and carers reported that having sufficient financial or other resources enabled them to provide additional help in the form of educational resources at home or direct support in the school and facilitated support from appropriate community organisations.

Within the context of transitions, this study raises wider issues concerning the extent to which young people's transitions reflect continuing outcomes of structural inequality rather than personal agency or choice. For the young people in this study, adolescence was the time when they were at greater risk of experiencing exclusion from school. This coincides with the time when they are making choices about the curriculum that have to be followed until they are at least 16 and, for most, 18 years old. Difficulties experienced at school at the beginning of this period can then set the young person on a path that they may find impossible to change. This could be avoided by creating a different type of institution that caters for the needs of young people at that time when they are maturing into adults.

Support, networks and resourcing

As highlighted in the case studies and in previous chapters, informal community networks, community-based initiatives, parents' associations and family played a crucial role in helping the young people overcome school exclusion. The testimonies of the young people in our sample suggest that an overriding concern for them in their schooling experience was to be listened to and to have their point of view heard, if not respected. Significantly, the experience of the young people in school and the quality of the relationship with teachers that in many instances triggered their exclusion were in sharp contrast to their experience outside school. Outside school, they engaged with the resources that constituted their social and cultural capital in their efforts to overcome school exclusions and make the transition to adulthood. These were sympathetic teachers, significant others, alternative sites of education and schooling, and family and friends.

It has long been the experience of voluntary education projects in the African-Caribbean community that children who come to them, having been excluded by mainstream schools and thought to be unteachable or uncontrollable, form constructive relationships with adults, develop a positive attitude to learning and become much more confident communicators. These changes lead to favourable educational outcomes, an accelerated rate of self-development and high levels of attainment. A key function of those projects, as we see from this study, has been to help young people prepare for readmission to school, after exclusion, by developing strategies for surviving schooling.

Many of the organisations and agencies involved in providing service to the young people did not have a remit to do so. However, these agencies were found to operate a 'holding function'. They also acted as a surrogate for the lack of statutory sector provision, filled the vacuum created by the shortcomings of statutory service provision and acted as a further safeguard for young people at risk of social exclusion. The voluntary sector's involvement in transition and education work highlights a need for statutory organisations and funders, such as regeneration and the Learning Skills Council, to provide support for capacity building to voluntary sector organisations working with young black people.

In recent years, there have been government-inspired programmes such as Connexions, the New Deal for Young People, Positive Futures and proposals from the Learning and Skills Council for extending learning grants for those over 19. It is argued that these programmes have failed to identify and address specific needs of young black people and in particular those excluded from school (DfES, 2003b). Over the years, it has been recognised that the local authority Youth Service has a crucial role to play in supporting young people (John, 1970). Several sources assert the need for the strengthening of the role of the Youth Service in working with youth people (e.g. DfES, 2003e). Yet, it is also argued that the consequence of government-inspired programmes such as Connexions is a reduction of the traditional youth service provision and its role in supporting young people (London Development Agency, 2004).

Policy recommendations

Based on the findings of this study, this final chapter provides a number of policy recommendations to the Department for Education and Skills (DfES), the Commission for Racial Equality (CRE), local education authorities (LEAs)/local authorities, further education colleges and institutions of higher education, schools and the black communities/black voluntary sector, which it is hoped will provide an impetus for change and improvement in line with national priorities and developments in a number of areas related to exclusionary processes and transitions.

Department for Education and Skills (DfES)

1   Although there have been nationally systemised school exclusion procedures in place for 18 years, the school exclusion rate for young people of African-Caribbean background remains disproportionably high. The DfES needs to work towards a policy of total non-exclusion.

2   Guidance and training modules should be produced on the use of Circular 10/99 in averting school exclusions. Proper implementation of its recommendations would enable all pupils to remain in mainstream schooling and ensure the reintegration of pupils if exclusion somehow proved necessary.

3   Funding must be made available for the training of everybody involved in the exclusion process to ensure greater awareness of the way race mediates the relationship between teacher and pupil.

4   School admissions, especially in relation to pupils experiencing problems, need to be transparent and accountable. Placement panels should have the power to direct schools to accept pupils, ensuring that their transitional needs are fully met. It is essential to provide empowering, congenial conditions for learning and all-round confident human development.

Commission for Racial Equality (CRE)

1   The CRE should give greater priority to assisting individual complainants from the black communities and to initiating formal investigations into high-excluding schools and authorities with demonstrable patterns of racial discrimination.

Local education authorities (LEAs)/local authorities

1   LEAs and local authorities should work with schools to ensure that robust strategies are put in place to reduce school exclusion and to comply with the Race Relations (Amendment) Act 2000 to tackle discrimination and disadvantage in this area.

2   They should effectively monitor arrangements for the excluded pupil to receive schoolwork pending the resolution of an appeal in cases of permanent exclusion, and ensure that the arrangements recognise the pupil's immediate and ongoing educational entitlement.

3   Many pupils complain about their mistreatment in schools either by teachers or peers. Parents are also concerned about what appear to them to be unfair practices. There should be a nationally agreed local complaints system, in which parents should have access to independent advocates, to resolve such problems.

4   There needs to be ongoing integrated support for excluded pupils to ensure successful reintegration, and careers advice and guidance either at the excluding school or elsewhere in the mainstream.

5   The Youth Service must be included in re-engaging young people encountering significant problems in education, as a response to preventing or mitigating social exclusion.

6   Local authorities should facilitate partnership working with the black voluntary sector for identifying and understanding the needs of African-Caribbean young people and to benefit from their ability to engage successfully with young people from these communities. It is important that this partnership is given due recognition and funded accordingly.

7   Nobody should be allowed to adjudicate a fixed-term or permanent exclusion without full, regular and up-to-date training in all the relevant legislation, including Circular 10/99, human rights and race relations. Similarly governing body and independent appeal clerks should have up-to-date legal experience.

8   Adjudicating bodies should contain at least one person from the same ethnic group and of the same sex as the excluded pupil, and on occasion should contain a majority or be wholly black and female.

9   Resources should be allocated to provide parents and pupils with independent advocate services.

10 In accordance with the Green Paper *Every Child Matters* (Her Majesty's Government, 2003), the Children's Bill now before Parliament attempts to secure better outcomes for excluded young people prone to social exclusion, risk and vulnerability. This could be achieved through support for partnership working between different agencies and through a dynamic programme to develop schools as accessible, open, inclusive, integrated, welcoming and accountable learning communities, capable of meeting the challenges of diversity, sudden population movements and changes, and catering for individual and community needs under one roof. They should have governing bodies, staffing, pupil enrolment, parents and community participation, curricula and teaching resources reflecting modern British society in an increasingly interdependent world. Training needs to be provided for all parties accordingly and progress needs to be monitored regularly.

Schools

1   Schools should have robust strategies in place, informed by the parameters of the Race Relations (Amendment) Act 2000, to address school exclusion. This is particularly important where school exclusion may serve to discriminate and disadvantage black pupils (see recommendation 1 under heading 'Commission for Racial Equality' and recommendation 1 under 'Local education authorities (LEAs)/local authorities' above).

2   There should be clearly written policies and procedures as to what types and incidence of behaviour would usually lead to permanent exclusion. These should be made known to all pupils, parents and carers (see recommendation 2 under heading 'Department for Education and Skills' above).

3   Genuine partnership must be facilitated with parents and the wider black community to ensure ongoing constructive dialogue between home and school, enable the early resolution of difficulties and avoid the need for the school to resort to a permanent exclusion.

Further education colleges and institutions of higher education

1   Further education colleges and universities need to reflect on their admission policies and procedures, and their equal opportunities policy and support structures available for black African-Caribbean applicants, given the possible experiences they may have had at school.

Black communities/black voluntary sector

1   Black communities need to support, safeguard and expand the community-based organisations that are available to parents and young people as a means of supporting parents to ensure the delivery of children's right to education. Further, the services should also constitute the means of empowering families in guiding and supporting their children in the future.

2   They should help to build independent organisations of parents and young people, which could act in their own interests and in support of the interests of teachers and schools in seeking to change the structure and processes of schooling and the world of education that so evidently produce such casualties within specific black and ethnic groups.

Notes

Chapter 1

1   In recent years, there have been an increasing number of studies examining the education of young African-Caribbean people and the role of school exclusion (e.g Wright *et al.*, 2000; Majors, 2001).

2   For example, in relation to crime, about a half of all school-age offenders have been excluded from school. In London, 40 per cent of robberies, 25 per cent of burglaries and 20 per cent of criminal damage are committed by 10–16 year olds (Greater London Authority, 2002). However, other studies (e.g. Home Office, 2000) noted that it is not possible to draw clear-cut causal links between school exclusion and offending. Where offending followed exclusion, there was often a significant time lag. However, the results suggest that maturation and the development of criminal careers were influential in the relationship between exclusion and offending. Excludees whose offending began before exclusion tended to be older at the point of permanent exclusion and the excludees whose offending began after exclusion tended to be younger.

3   http://www.DfES.gov.uk/thelearninggateway.

4   'Black' as used in this report refers to those of African and African-Caribbean heritage. The Department for Education and Skills (DfES) term 'black Caribbean' is equivalent to the term 'African Caribbean'.

5   It is not clear from these figures whether they include individuals who have been excluded more than once. However, it is recognised that Nottingham excludes at a rate of 22 per 10,000 compared with a national average of 12 and 10 per 10,000 in the County of Nottinghamshire. Its primary rate is over three times the national average and its secondary rate much higher at 43 per 10,000 compared with 27 nationally.

Chapter 4

1   This is to be expected given the way the sample was selected (see Chapter 5).

Bibliography

Ahier, J. and Moore, R. (1999) 'Post-16 education, semi-dependent youth and privatisation of interage transfers: re-theorising youth transition', *British Journal of Sociology of Education*, Vol. 20, No. 4, pp. 514–30

Allen, D. (2002) ' Research involving vulnerable young people: a discussion of ethical and methodological concerns', *Drugs: Education, Prevention and Policy*, Vol. 9, No. 3, pp. 275–83

Alleyne, B. (2002) *Radicals against Race*. Oxford: Berg

Appiah, L. (2001) *Mentoring: School–Business Links*. London: The Runnymede Trust

Blair, M. (2001) *Why Pick on Me?* Stoke-on-Trent: Trentham Books

Brah, A. (1992) 'Diversity, difference and differentiation', in J. Donald and A. Rattansi (eds) *Race, Culture and Difference*. London: Sage

Bourdieu, P. (1986) 'The forms of capital', in J.G. Richardson (ed.) *Handbook of Theory and Research for the Sociology of Education*. New York: Greenwood Press

Bynner, J. (2001) 'British youth transitions in comparative perspective', *Journal of Youth Studies*, Vol. 4. No. 1, pp. 5–23

Clark, A. and Moss, P. (2001) *Listening to Young Children: The Mosaic Approach*. London: National Children's Bureau

Cohen, R. and Hughes, M. with Ashworth, L. and Blair, M. (1994) *School's out: The Family Perspective on School Exclusion*. Essex: Family Service Unit

Craig, G. (2002) *Reaching Disaffected Youth*. Lincoln: Lincolnshire TEC

CRE (Commission for Racial Equality) (1997) *Exclusion from School and Racial Equality*. London: CRE

DfEE (Department for Education and Employment) (1999a) *Social Inclusion: Pupil Support*. Circular 10/99. London: DfEE

DfEE (Department for Education and Employment) (1999b) *Social Inclusion: The LEA Role in Pupil Support.* Circular 11/99. London: DfEE

DfEE (Department for Education and Employment) (2000a) *Statistics of Education, Permanent Exclusions from Maintained Schools in England (10/00).* London: DfEE

DfEE (Department for Education and Employment) (2000b) *Connexions: Connexions Service Prospectus and Specification.* London: DfEE

DfEE (Department for Education and Employment) (2000c) *Connexions: The Best Start in Life for Every Young Person.* London: DfEE

DfES (Department for Education and Skills) (2003a) *Statistics of Education, Permanent Exclusions from Schools and Exclusion Appeals, England 2001/2002 (Provisional).* London: DfES

DfES (Department for Education and Skills) (2003b) *Minority Ethnic Attainment and Participation in Education and Training: The Evidence.* Research topic paper RTP01-03. London: DfES

DfES (Department for Education and Skills) (2003c) *Aiming High: Raising the Achievement of Minority Ethnic Pupils (0183/2003).* London: DfES

DfES (Department for Education and Skills) (2003d) *Minority Ethnic Students in Higher Education: Interim Report.* London: DfES

DfES (Department for Education and Skills) (2003e) *Transforming Youth Work Resourcing Excellent Youth Services.* London: DfES

DfES (Department for Education and Skills) (2004) *Permanent Exclusions from Schools and Exclusion Appeals, England 2002/2003 (Provisional).* London: DfES

Dove, N. (1993) 'The emergence of black supplementary schools: resistance to racism in the United Kingdom', *Urban Education*, Vol. 27, No. 2, pp. 43–57

Dove, N. (1998) *Afrikan Mothers: Bearers of Culture, Makers of Social Change.* New York: Albany

German, G. (2001) 'Inclusivity, integration and integrity', in ROTA CEN (eds) *Inclusivity, Integration and Integrity.* London: ROTA

Gillborn, D. and Gipps, C. (1996) *Recent Research on the Achievement of Ethnic Minority Pupils*. London: HMSO

Gillborn, D. and Mirza, H. (2000) *Mapping Class, Gender and Race*. London: Ofsted

Graham, J. and Bowling, B. (1995) *Young People and Crime*. Home Office Research Study No. 145. London: HMSO

Greater London Authority (2002) *London Divided – Income Inequality and Poverty in the Capital*. London: Greater London Authority

Green, E., Mitchell, W. and Burton, R. (2001) 'Contextualising risk and danger: an analysis of young people's perception of risk', *Journal of Youth Studies*, Vol. 3, No. 2, pp. 10–35

Harris, N. and Eden, K. with A. Blair (2000) *Challenges to School Exclusion: Exclusion; Appeals; the Law*. London: Routledge

Hayden, C. (1996) 'Excluded from primary school', *Representing Children*, Vol. 9, No. 4, pp. 199–209

Hayden, C. (1997) *Children Excluded from Primary School: Debates, Evidence, Responses*. Buckingham: Open University Press

Hayden, C. and Dunne, S. (2001) *Outside Looking In: Children and Families' Experience of Social Exclusion*. London: The Children's Society

Her Majesty's Government (2003) *Every Child Matters*. Green Paper. London: The Stationery Office

Home Office (2000) *The Independent Effects of Permanent Exclusion from School on the Offending Careers of Young People*. London: Home Office

Home Office (2002) *Black and Minority Ethnic Voluntary and Community Organisations: A Code of Good Practice – Compact on Relations between Government and the Voluntary and Community Sector in England*. London: Home Office, Active Community Unit

Howes, E. (2003) *2001 Census Key Statistics: Ethnicity, Religion and Country of Birth*. DMAG Briefing 2003/9. London: Greater London Authority

Hughes, M., Wikely, F. and Nash, T. (1994) *Parents and their Children's Schools.* London: Blackwell.

John, G. (1970) *Race in the Inner-city: A Report for Handsworth.* London: Runnymede Trust

Jones, G. (2002) *The Youth Divide: Diverging Paths to Adulthood.* York: Joseph Rowntree Foundation.

Jones, L. (1984) 'White–black achievement differences', *American Sociological Review,* Vol. 39, No. 11, pp. 1207–13

Kelly, P. and Kenway, J. (2001) 'Managing youth transitions in the network society', *British Journal of Sociology of Education,* Vol. 22, No. 1, pp. 19–33

London Development Agency (2004) *The Educational Experiences and Achievements of Black Boys in London Schools 2000–2003. A Report by the Education Commission.* London: London Development Agency

Macrae, S., Maguire, M. and Melbourne, L. (2003) 'Social exclusion: exclusion from school', *International Journal of Inclusive Education,* Vol. 7, No. 2, pp. 89–101

Majors, R. (ed.) (2001) *Educating our Black Children: New Directions and Radical Approaches.* London: Routledge Falmer Press

Marshall, F., Ardon, R. and Truin, P. (2003) *Hard to Reach Groups: Young People: A Case Study of Radford & Hyson Green NDC.* Nottingham: New Deal For Communities National Evaluation

Milne, A., Myers, D., Rosenthal, A. and Ginsburg, A. (1986) 'Single parents, working mothers, and the educational achievement of school children', *Sociology of Education,* Vol. 59, No. 3, pp. 125–39

Mirza, H.S. (1992) *Young, Female and Black.* London: Routledge

Mirza, H.S and Reay, D. (2000) 'Spaces and places of black educational desire: rethinking black supplementary schools as a new social movement', *Sociology,* Vol. 34, No. 3, pp. 521–44

Nottingham City Council Education Department (2002) *Exclusion from Secondary Schools (2001/2).* Nottingham: Nottingham City Council Education Department

Ofsted (1996) *Exclusion from Secondary Schools, 1995–96: A Report from HMCI.* London: The Stationery Office

Ofsted (2001) *Improving Attendance and Behaviour in Secondary Schools.* London: Ofsted

Orr, A.J. (2003) 'Black–white differences in achievement: the importance of wealth', *Sociology of Education*, Vol. 76, No. 4, pp. 281–304

Osler, A. (1997) *Exclusion from School and Racial Equality.* London: CRE

Osler, A. and Hill, J. (1999) 'Exclusion from school and racial equality: an examination of government proposals in light of recent research evidence', *Cambridge Journal of Education*, Vol. 29, No. 1

Osler, A., Street, C., Lall, M. and Vincent, C. (2002) *Girls and School Exclusion.* York: Joseph Rowntree Foundation

Parsons, C. (1999) *Education, Exclusion and Citizenship.* London: Routledge

Parsons, C. and Castle, F. (1999) 'The economics of exclusion', in C. Parsons (ed.) *Education, Exclusion and Citizenship.* London: Routledge

Parsons, C., Benns, L., Hailes, J. and Howlett, K. (1994) *Excluding Primary School Children.* London: Family Policy Studies Centre/Joseph Rowntree Foundation

Parsons, C., Castle, F., Hawlett, K. and Worrall, J. (1996) *Exclusion from School: The Public Cost.* London: Commission for Racial Equality

Pomeroy, E. (2000) *Experiencing Exclusion.* Stoke on Trent: Trentham Books

Putnam, R.D. (1995) 'Bowling alone: America's declining social capital', *Journal of Democracy*, Vol. 6, No. 1, pp. 65–78

Reay, D. (2000) 'A useful extension of Bourdieu's conceptual framework? Emotional capital as a way of understanding mothers' involvement in their children's education?', *Sociological Review*, Vol. 30, No. 5, pp. 545–58

Reay, D. and Mirza, H. (1997) 'Uncovering the genealogies of the margins: black supplementary schools', *British Journal of Sociology of Education*, Vol. 18, No. 4, pp. 477–99

Reynolds, T. (2001) 'Black mothering, paid work and identity', *Ethnic and Racial Studies*, Vol. 24, No. 6, pp. 1046–64

Rhamie, J. and Hallam, S. (2002) 'An investigation into African-Caribbean academic success in the UK', *Race Ethnicity and Education*, Vol. 5, No. 2, pp. 130–45

Rudd, P. and Evans, K. (1998) 'Structure and agency in youth transitions: students' experience of vocational education', *Journal of Youth Studies*, Vol. 1, No. 1, pp. 39–63

Scott-Jones, D. and Turner, S. (1990) 'The impact of adolescent childrearing on educational attainment and income of black females', *Youth and Society*, Vol. 22, No. 1, pp. 2–28

SEU (Social Exclusion Unit) (1999) *Truancy and School Exclusion*. London: The Stationery Office

Sewell, T. (1997) *Black Masculinities and Schooling: How Black Boys Survive Modern Schooling*. Stoke on Trent: Trentham Books Ltd

Sewell, T. (2004) 'Taking a stand', BBC Radio 4, 27 January

Smith, A. and Osbourn, M. (2003) 'Interpretative phenomenological analysis', in J.A. Smith (ed.) *Qualitative Psychology: A Practical Guide to Research Methods*. London: Sage

Thomson, R., Bell, R., Holland, J., Henderson, S., McGrellis, S. and Sharpe, S. (2002) 'Critical moments: choice, chance and opportunity in young people's narratives of transition, *Sociology*, Vol. 36, No. 2, pp. 335–53

Thomson, R., Henderson, S. and Holland, J. (2003) 'Making the most of what you've got? Resources, values and inequalities in young women's transitions to adulthood', *Educational Review*, Vol. 55, No. 1, pp. 33–46

Weekes, D. and Wright, C. (1998) *Improving Practice: A Whole School Approach To Raising the Achievement of African Caribbean Youth*. London: The Runnymede Trust

Wright, C., Weekes, D. and McGlaughlin, A. (2000) *'Race', Class and Gender in Exclusion from School*. London: Falmer Press

Wright, C., Weekes, D., McGlaughlin, A. and Webb, D. (1998) 'Masculinised discourses within education and the construction of black male identities amongst African-Caribbean youth', *British Journal of Sociology of Education*, Vol. 19, No. 1, pp. 75–87

Youth Justice Board (2003) *Youth Survey – Research Study Conducted for the Youth Justice Board by Mori, January-March 2003.* London: Youth Justice Board

Appendix 1: Details of the young people interviewed for the study

Table A1.1 Ethnic background

Ethnic background	No. of young people
Both parents black African-Caribbean	25
One parent black African-Caribbean and one white-British parent	8
Total	33

Table A1.2 Number of previous exclusions experienced by the young people

No. of exclusions	No. of young people
1	2
2	2
3	15
4	4
5+	4
Unknown	6
Total	33

Table A1.3 Age at final exclusion

Age at final exclusion	No. of young people
London	
13	0
14	5
15	14
16	1
17	0
Nottingham	
13	5
14	5
15	3
16	0
17	0

Table A1.4 Living arrangements

Living arrangements	No. of young people
Both parents	9
Single parent	15
Other relatives	2
Care/hostel	7
Total	33

Table A1.5 Types of schools excluded from

Type of school excluded from	No. of young people
City technical college	1
Single-sex school	1
Roman Catholic/Catholic school	6
Private fee-paying school	1
Community secondary school/secondary school	24
Total	33

Figure A1.1 Age of young people by gender

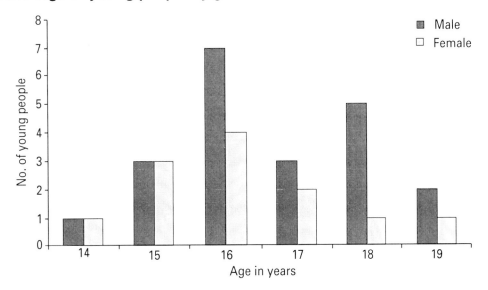

Appendix 2: Details of the interviews completed for the study

Nottingham interview set

The Nottingham interview set included:

- introductory (first) interviews with 13 young people

- six young people participated in the friendship group interviews based on photo stories

- 11 family members or carers (i.e. an identified social worker) were interviewed

- ten individuals (representing 16 voluntary organisations) from voluntary sector projects were interviewed and eight individuals from the statutory sector (including the Social Services, Youth Offending Team and from the Education Action Zone)

- final interviews with ten young people.

London interview set

The London interview set included:

- introductory (first) interviews with 20 young people; because of a delay in the recruitment to the project, the introductory and final interviews were combined for ten young people

- three young people participated in the friendship group interviews based on photo stories

- eight family members were interviewed

- interviews with three key individuals from the voluntary/community sector projects (i.e. CEN, ISSP and one Saturday school) and one key individual from the statutory sector (Connexions)

- final interviews with four young people.

Appendix 3: The young people's destinations

Table A3.1 Destination immediately following exclusion

Destination immediately following exclusion	No. of young people
Pupil Referral Unit	9
Mentoring project	4
Further education	3
(Other) school	12
Other	2
Unknown	3
Total	33

Table A3.2 Destination at time of interview

Destination at time of interview	No. of young people
Further education	22
Sixth form	1
Employment	4
Unemployed	3
Other	3
Unknown	0
Total	33

Appendix 4: Qualifications obtained at time of interview

Table A4.1 Qualifications obtained at time of interview

Qualifications obtained	No. of young people
GCSEs	11
General National Vocational Qualifications (GNVQs)	4
None	16
Unknown	2
Total	33

Appendix 5: Family members interviewed

Table A5.1 Family members interviewed

Young person	Location	Relationship to young person
Ray	Nottingham	Grandfather
Richard	Nottingham	Mother and father
Rose	Nottingham	Mother
Earl	Nottingham	Mother
Anthony	Nottingham	Mother
David	Nottingham	Mother
Keenan	Nottingham	Mother
Ria	Nottingham	Sister
Roger	London	Mother
Lee	London	Mother
Lucinda	London	Mother
Yolan	London	Mother
Kareen	London	Mother
Gavin	London	Mother
Tamara	London	Mother
Sirita	London	Mother

Appendix 6: National and local policy, programmes and support networks for young people

AACPAG (The African and African-Caribbean People's Advisory Group)
Head Office 0208 667 9222
ACNA Centre
31 Hungerhill Road
St Anns
Nottingham

The Advisory Centre for Education
1B Aberdeen Studios
22 Highbury Grove
London
N5 2DQ
0207 354 8318

African Caribbean Development Agency
New Brook House
385 Alfreton Road
Nottingham
NG7 5LR
0115 875 8846

African Caribbean Families and Friends (ACFF)
28 Beaconsfield Street,
Hyson Green
Nottingham
NG7 6FD

African Caribbean Family Support Project
The Croft
Albert Road
Alexandra Park
Nottingham
NG3 4JD
0115 962 0772

Black Families in Education
Hyson Green Community Centre
37a Gregory Boulevard
Hyson Green
Nottingham
NG7 6BE
0115 841 3896

BUILD Nottingham Mentor Programme
164 Alfreton Road
Nottingham
NG7 3NS
www.build2000.force9.co.uk

CEN (Communities Empowerment Network)
107 Trinity Road
London
SW17 7SQ
0208 767 5591 / 5670
www.compowernet.org

Calabash Supplementary School
The Pilgrim Church
Queens Walk/Houseman Gardens
The Meadows
Nottingham
NG2 2DF
0115 96 5633

Connexions Service
www.connexions.gov.uk

ERONDU
Radford Unity Complex
Radford
Nottingham
0115 9781673
Hyson Green Girls' Club
37a Gregory Boulevard
Nottingham
NG7 6BE

Hyson Green Youth Club
Hyson Green
Terrance Street
Nottingham

LIBRA
Radford Unity Complex
203 Ilkeston Road
Radford
Nottingham
0115 978 1673

The New Deal for Young People
www.thesite.org/newdeal

PATRA East Midlands Limited
Marcus Garvey Centre
Lenton Boulevard
Radford
Nottingham
NG7 2BV
0115 942 2440
www.patraeastmidlands.co.uk

Shiefton Youth Group
Radford Unity Complex
203 Ilkeston Road,
Radford
Nottingham
0115 9793118

SIMBA Education Ltd
ACFF Centre
28 Beaconsfield Street
Nottingham
NG7 6FD
Email: anne-simba@yahoo.co.uk
01159251025

Social Exclusion Unit
www.cabinet-office.gov.uk/seu